Wanderlust EDU

An Educator's Guide to Innovation, Change, and Adventure

by Micah Shippee, PhD

with illustrations *by* Chris Stein

For Laura, Bekah, Tripp, and Liberty
I love you.

For Jen and Tessa
Thank you.

WanderlustEDU

© 2019 by Micah Shippee
www.micahshippee.com

Published 2019 by EdTechTeam Press, Irvine, California.

ISBN-13: 978-1-945167-59-1

23 22 21 20 19   1 2 3 4 5

Illustrations by Chris Stein.

Cover and book design by Ignacio Huizar - www.nachohuizar.com.

Editing and project management by Justin Jaquith and Jaquith Creative.

This book is available at a discount when purchased in quantity for use as premiums, promotions, fundraising, or education. For inquiries, contact the publisher at press@edtechteam.com. Also available in e-book format.

Praise for WanderlustEDU

Micah is a true leader in innovation and emergent technology, but he also has both feet firmly planted in education. His years of teaching combined with his extensive research in innovation adoption make for a great mix of practical advice informed by solid educational theory. I highly recommend *WanderlustEDU* for anyone who wants to prepare their classroom or school for the future of education, as well as for anyone leading a book study group in the education space. I'm grateful to Micah for championing the value of innovation and technology not for their own sake, but the sake of our students and the future.

— Thomas C. Murray, Director of Innovation, Future Ready Schools, Washington, D.C.

WanderlustEDU is a challenging call for educators to grow, change, and innovate so we can provide the best possible education for our students. Thankfully it is also a helpful guide to lead us along each step of this journey.

— Eric Curts, Technology Integrationist, ControlAltAchieve.com

Micah Shippee leads us on the journey to developing an innovativeness mindset, which he describes as the "skill and imagination to create continually." Shippee provides the pedagogical reasoning and practical methods to help us take risks, iterate our practice, make meaningful use of technology, and learn to support our colleagues and schools as they move towards this same goal. Shippee's book is perfect for a PLC or book study for those who want to move ahead with change!

— Kathy Schrock, Educational Technologist

Having had the genuine pleasure of working closely with Micah to support the growth of leaders in embracing change through a culture of innovation, it is obvious *WanderlustEDU* is written from a perspective of knowing and doing. Micah's depth of knowledge in the adoption of emergent technologies is unmatched, yet his unassuming and light-hearted manner of delivering professional learning is both inviting and non-intimidating. Reflected in the pages of *WanderlustEDU* is the growth in understanding and knowledge that I have personally experienced in working with Micah as an educational leader. He exemplifies "innovativeness" in practice and sharing. Micah has provided a road map that will empower all learners to become innovators and encourage all leaders to disrupt education to impact school change positively.

— Simone Gessler, Assistant Superintendent of Learning, Yellowknife Catholic Schools

WanderlustEDU weaves together stories, metaphors, and research to inspire educators of all levels to innovate for the betterment of the students they serve. Micah provides practical tips and compelling arguments for integrating emergent technology into the learning experiences designed for both students and educators themselves.

— Katherine Goyette, Educational Technology and Integrated Studies Consultant

Micah is one of the most down to earth, clever, insightful, and passionate educators I have had the fortune to work with. He brings those same qualities to *WanderlustEDU*, which reminds all educators— both veteran and novice—that teaching and learning are about the journey and inspiring curiosity in both ourselves and our students, as opposed to focusing on the destination (the test or the grade). Micah cleverly addresses many key topics to inspire meaningful change, including culture shifts and designing quality professional learning, throughout the book. *WanderlustEDU* will be your cheerleader when trying something new, providing you with a roadmap to innovation and iteration as you navigate your teaching journey!

— Katie Ritter, Director of Curriculum and Technology Integration, Forward Edge

Table of Contents

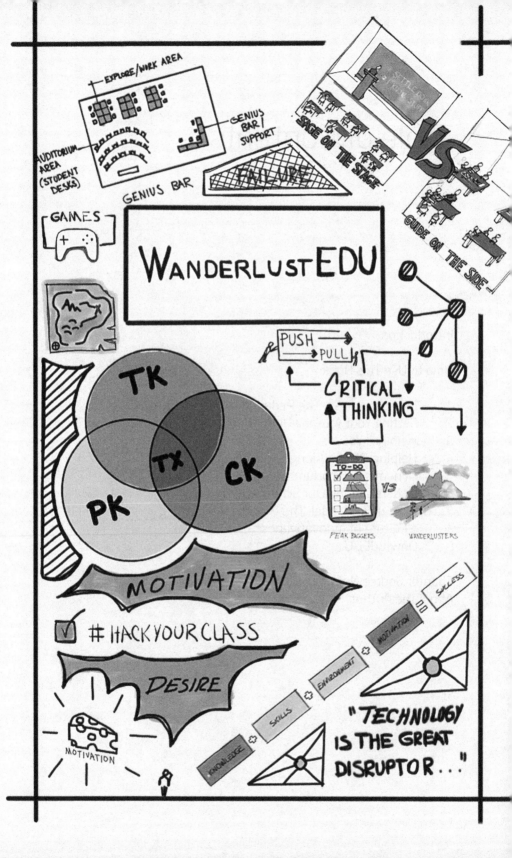

Introduction

It's the sides of the mountain which sustain life, not the top.
—Robert M. Pirsig

Travel isn't always pretty. It isn't always comfortable. Sometimes it hurts, it even breaks your heart. But that's okay. The journey changes you; it should change you. It leaves marks on your memory, on your consciousness, on your heart, and on your body. You take something with you. Hopefully, you leave something good behind.
–Anthony Bourdain

Have you ever taken a trip that turned into more of an adventure than you originally planned? I don't mean the destination was an adventure: I mean the *trip itself,* the getting from Point A to Point B. Maybe an incorrect itinerary, lost luggage, wrong directions, or "interesting" people contributed to an unexpected travel experience. Later, when someone asked you, "How was your trip?" you quickly rattled off the list of the crazy things that happened and how they took away from the travel experience.

Why do we often let mishaps like these bother us, rather than focusing on an otherwise positive overall experience? I think the issue is our perspective. We're used to viewing travel as a necessary evil to get to a fun destination. The trip is about the arrival, not about the journey. So, if anything goes wrong on the way, it throws us off mentally and emotionally.

1

But contrast the concept of a *trip* to somewhere with that of a *journey through* somewhere. Imagine road tripping across the US, backpacking through Southeast Asia, or making some other meandering, wandering journey. If you've ever taken a trip like that, you know the adventure is not just in the destination, but in the journey. You assume beforehand there will be complicated moments along the way, so you approach the whole experience expecting the unexpected. Little things don't bother you as much. You become less stressed about where you are going or what might go wrong. You become accustomed to solving problems, plotting new courses, navigating detours. And along the way, you have the time of your life. Instead of complaining about your crazy traveling experiences, you almost brag about them. And perhaps more importantly, you grow. You learn new skills. You become a bigger person with a larger worldview and a greater capacity to manage change.

Now let's apply the difference between a trip and a journey to education. Do you remember why you got into education in the first place? To make a real difference in lives. To help people. To shape culture. To empower kids. To change generations and communities. To break cycles of poverty. And so much more! Those are beautiful and worthy goals. But if you don't have the right view of the educational experience, you might view the day-to-day challenges and learning curve of your job as obstacles in the way of arriving at your destination. Long-term, you can end up resisting innovation, adaptation, and growth because these things imply risk and change.

It's easy to lose the joy of the educational adventure when we're so focused on little roadblocks along the way or things that might go wrong in the future. I'm talking about things like schedules, equipment problems, school policies, other teachers, parents, budgets, professional development requirements, new technology, new theories of education, and more. If we view these as problems that spoil our teaching experience, we'll overlook the adventure found in the process.

I'd like to suggest that we reframe our teaching goals and experience in the context of journey. Rather than arriving at work hoping for as few problems as possible, what if we showed up with a sense of adventure? Rather than making a mental list of all the negative things that could happen, what if we took pride in our ability to innovate and adapt? What if we looked at the future—with its ups and downs, its trials and errors, its rewards and disappointments, its roadblocks and detours—as an exciting set of unknowns that we are more than capable of facing successfully?

That's where the word *wanderlust* comes in. Webster's defines wanderlust as "an impulse, longing, or urge to wander or travel."[1] It's a term that refers to an innate sense of adventure, a willingness to explore the unknown. For me, this word encompasses the educator's challenge and calling, which is to continually adapt, grow, and innovate in order to provide the best teaching experience for his or her students. I want to show you why this approach toward life is necessary to a fulfilling career.

This book explores innovation in the teaching practice, but my goal is not to add more to your already-full schedule. It's not to overwhelm you or criticize you because you aren't adapting fast enough. I want to give you *hope* and I want to give you a *map*, and for me, both of those things are a direct result of learning to embrace the adventure inherent in being a professional educator. As a veteran teacher and qualitative researcher, I have learned to love the power of exploring life as a journey, a truly disruptive saga, a story that unfolds as we find new and better ways to face the educational challenge.

Educators aren't first teachers: we are first *learners*, because we have to learn what we are going to teach and also how best to teach it. We are explorers, adventurers, pioneers. We are constantly experimenting and continually innovating. If we can cultivate an attitude of educational wanderlust, we will be much better prepared to embrace (rather than resist) the adventures that come with ever-adapting technology, changing educational strategies, and other shifts in our field.

It has often been said that life is a journey, not a destination. While I agree with the focus on journey and process, destinations are important. Directionless wandering is not fulfilling or effective. Destinations, in the form of goals, provide us with compass-like guidance. On our journey through life, therefore, we must focus on the *waypoints*, not just the endpoint.

This wanderlust approach to our educational calling will serve our students better than a change-resistant approach, because as educators, we concern ourselves with the impact the *future* will have on our students. We are preparing our students for what lies ahead. In the future, robots, rather than traditional workers, may do much of what humans used to do. Traditional manual labor skills are being transformed through software and hardware advancements. No one really knows the speed at which this workforce-shift will occur, only that it is already happening. If we model change and adaptation in teaching, we teach our students to adapt to change in the world around them.

Change can be both unsettling and exciting. It takes effort to embrace new things and to pursue shifts in our educational paradigm that best support our students for their future. When we're already feeling maxed out just trying to juggle our current teaching and homework load, the extra work involved with learning a new method or technology and then incorporating it into our teaching can be daunting and demotivating. That creates a negative cycle, though, because inwardly, we know we need to adapt and learn. We feel like we're falling further behind. That can bring an additional load of frustration, insecurity, and even guilt, as we start to feel like the world is moving too fast for us to keep up.

The good news is that innovation and exploration are not reserved for a few super-intelligent, technology-adept individuals. All of us can innovate, and all of us *must*. I would argue that educators, by definition, are uniquely equipped to innovate. We are good at this. Teachers have been innovating for years, decades, centuries, millennia. Education has always had one foot in the past, honoring and preserving truth; and one foot in the future, inspiring students to build on what they have received using tools they will probably help invent.

Let's embrace the process and enjoy the journey. Let's set and celebrate clear waypoints rather than stressing about the time it takes to reach them. Let's face new students, new technologies, new social media channels, new administrations, new theories, new textbooks, new budgets, and new *anything* with this solid conviction: *I can do this. I was made for this. I have more to offer my students than ever before, and these changes only make me more effective than ever.*

Innovation in school begins with the concept of choice for change. Do we change because we are told to or because we decide to? Choosing to travel versus being forced to travel will create a very different experience. We will talk about terms like adoption and integration, because adoption implies the power to choose, whereas integration can infer a change forced upon us.

Ultimately, we want to be not just innovative individuals, but innovative schools. We will take a look at some of the ways we can help create cultures conducive to innovation and adoption. Whether your sphere is that of teacher or administrator, you will find practical explanations about how to bring others along on your journey.

My stories, explanations, and challenges to you come from over two decades of experience as a classroom teacher and technology coach, as well as from extensive (and passionate) academic research. I have taken the research deep-dive in the fields of educational technology, instructional design, and the diffusion of innovation. The latter was the basis for my PhD dissertation, "mLearning in the Organizational Innovation Process," which explored how individuals and organizations innovate via mobile learning (known as mLearning, for short).[2] Specifically, I analyzed mobile learning as an innovation centered on pedagogy (teaching courses on a phone) that occurs through the deployment of emergent technology (smartphones).

The qualitative data collection in my dissertation took a year because I chose to use a methodology called a *longitudinal case study*. That is, I wanted to know the whole story, with all of its facets: the people, the choices, the successes, the failures. That comprehensive work is the basis for much of what I have learned and what I share in the following pages.

While researching my thesis, I began to see technology as a *type* of innovation, rather than the *definition* of innovation. Yet, it also became clear to me that most of us can understand the changes caused by innovating when we have a physical object (such as some form of emergent technology) to guide our discussion. Therefore, much of the book is framed around emergent technology as a tangible example we can all relate to due to its undeniable impact on education.

There are countless types of innovation, and technology is only one of them. If tech is a bit intimidating to you, that should be reassuring; because odds are, you are a very innovative person in many areas. Innovation often includes technology, but it is not limited to it. The goal is not to become "techies," but to become innovators. And along the way, I'm confident you'll discover tech-related innovation to be easier and more productive than you might have thought.

How do I hope to go about this, especially since your role in your school or district is unique and specific to you? First, *teachers* will find encouragement and useful strategies to support the adoption of innovation at the grassroots level. Second, *decision-makers* on all levels will be challenged to look at their effectiveness in adopting innovation. Third, *education leaders and administrators* will see that innovativeness transcends the latest and greatest technology and speaks to a powerful change in school culture.

In short, all of us will see where, when, and how we can change ourselves and become agents of change for others. By embracing the adventures on our teaching journey, we can make a difference at every level of education.

Let's do this!

Micah

How to Use This Book

In each chapter, I will explore specific topics, theories, and methodologies that intersect with the teaching process. Along the way, I will provide several *waypoints* and *signposts* to guide you.

Waypoints

Any long journey will include regular navigational stops. These are often called *waypoints*, and they are always a good idea. It is in these pauses that we reflect, assess, and plan. Are we still on the right track? Do we need to change course a bit? Do we need to map out a whole new course? I will provide you with *waypoints* for the same purpose—as a place to stop, reflect, and plan for your adventure.

Signposts

Long journeys also include many *signposts*, signs that guide us and give directions. They are a necessary component for a successful journey because they help distinguish where we are, where we have been, and where we are going. At the end of each chapter, we will create signposts to help guide us on our journey. Our signposts will aid our understanding of what has happened at each point and better direct where we are going next.

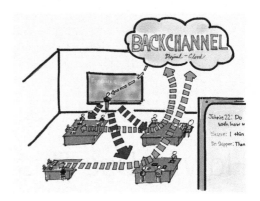

Backchanneling

The practice of using devices to maintain an online conversation alongside a conference, activity, or event is sometimes called *backchanneling*.

Participants or attendees use sites or social media, like Twitter, to discuss the event as it is happening in real time. Often this is done by "tagging" other users, "geotagging" a specific location, or "hashtagging" a key term.

Besides learning from what others find important, one big benefit of backchanneling is growing your Personal Learning Network (PLN). Your PLN refers to the people and resources you learn from, usually informally, in order to grow as an educator. Twitter happens to be my favorite means of interacting with and expanding my PLN, but many other social media and online sources can do the same.

As you read this book, feel free to engage with me (@micahshippee) and other readers through backchanneling. Here are some suggestions:

- When you post, tweet, or share a pic, use the hashtag #wanderlustEDU to find others who are on this journey with you.
- Games of all kinds in education are valuable tools to promote engagement and learning. Share your favorite use of games in education with #gamingEDU.
- Use #hackyourclass to find or share inspiration regarding creative ways to use your learning spaces, such as an innovative classroom layout or a dream-sketch of the perfect classroom.

Finally, visit bit.ly/WanderlustEDU to download a copy of the *Wanderlust EDU Book Companion*, which contains the waypoints and signposts from this book in a convenient, printable format.

Innovativeness: the Pedagogy of the Future

Don't adventures ever have an end? I suppose not.
Someone else always has to carry on the story.
—J.R.R. Tolkein

I n our journey as educators, we strive to start with the skills and knowledge loaded into our brains and backpacks that will best benefit our students. But starting right is not enough. Any prolonged journey requires that we periodically restock our supplies, refine our plans, and acquire whatever information or tools are needed for the next stage. The same holds true for the teaching journey. We teach from a place of constant change because the world is constantly changing.

The key to a successful journey as educators is to develop an iterative approach to thinking, something called *innovativeness*. Granted, that word does not exactly roll off the tongue; but it simply refers to the quality of being innovative. It encompasses both the actions and the underlying mindset of an educator. Innovativeness is the skill and imagination to create continually. It is a philosophy that embraces change and recognizes the flexibility necessary to prepare for an uncertain, moving-target future. An innovative teacher is willing to try new things in the classroom and to embrace failure as a learning opportunity. An innovative school fosters a culture where trying new things is the status quo. Innovativeness, therefore, is the pedagogy of the future.

An important myth to bust is that emergent technology is a synonym for innovation. *It is not.* I can't stress that enough. Think of innovation as a boundless and continuous road trip and technology (in terms of education) as a vehicle we use to get around. New technology can be a part of innovation, but it is not the dot on the map that says you've arrived.

So What Is Innovation?

Innovation, in and of itself, is simply something new. An innovation may be developed from something already in existence (e.g. those prehistoric-looking cell phones made way for the small, slim devices we have now), or it can be something totally new (e.g. Airbnb and Uber). With that definition in mind, we can talk about innovation in schools in reference to a new math teaching program, a fresh approach to discussion in our humanities courses, or a new device for analysis in science classes. It's all innovation.

When we add innovations to our teacher toolkits—or to our metaphorical backpacks, using wanderlust terminology—those supplies enrich and empower our journey. But keep in mind, they don't define it indefinitely. That's worth emphasizing.

Falling in love with our methods and our tools can be treacherous if we get stuck in our comfort zone. That doesn't mean you won't have favorite, tried-and-true teaching tools, of course; but always be open to upgrading to something more appropriate to the task. A skilled educator is able to adapt or upgrade those tools when the need demands, without losing himself or herself in the process. Your effectiveness isn't defined by one method or one tool, but by the ever-increasing sum of the things you gather along the way.

Innovativeness, therefore, is the most essential thing to pack on your educational journey. It is the quality that will allow you to assimilate new learning and face new challenges while maintaining the essence of who you are and what you set out to accomplish. Innovativeness is truly the pedagogy of the future.

Defining Technology

While technology is not synonymous with innovation, it's important to examine and talk about it because of the sizable role it plays in innovation. Discoveries and advances in the technical fields of communications, science, electronics, and computing are currently happening at incredible speeds and have vast applications in our students' lives and in our teaching. Maybe we should stop and ask ourselves, what exactly is this "technology" thing we are talking about? To understand technology as a whole, it's helpful to recognize the nebulous use of the term up front and distinguish some of its parts.

In educational use today, technology often refers to computers, software, or anything with buttons, LED screens, or internet connectivity. So when we talk about technology in the rest of this book, that is typically what we are referencing.

That is a fairly specific use of the term, however. In the overall progress of history, technology has a broader definition. The dictionary defines it as "the practical application of knowledge, especially in a particular area."[3] In other words, whenever we take technical knowledge from any field and use it to solve a problem or address a need, we are using technology. For example, a prosthetic leg is a device that solves a problem by replacing a limb. There are no buttons, screens, or connectivity, yet it is technology.

Furthermore, the definition I quoted above goes on to clarify that technology often transcends a physical object—referring instead to processes, methods, and knowledge involved in accomplishing a task. In short, new technology might be an idea, thought, or workflow.

To complicate the idea even further, the term "technology" is often applied to something just because it is new. For example, there was a point in history when pencils were new, ground-breaking technology. The same goes for calculators and copy machines. We know these as familiar friends; they're old-school tools, but make no mistake, they are technological tools. They just happen to be technology that we are no longer intimidated by. (Well, copy machines can be intimidating, but only when they get jammed, but that is more infuriating than intimidating.) We'll talk more about some of these innovations below.

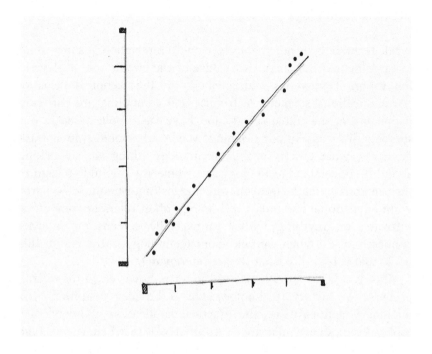

It should be clear to all of us that technology is here to stay. And not only are technological advancements not going away, they are increasing exponentially.

In 1965, Gordon Moore, co-founder of Intel, noticed that the number of transistors per square inch on integrated circuits had doubled every year since their invention. Moore developed a theory, commonly called Moore's Law, which predicts that this trend will continue into the foreseeable future, doubling every twenty-four months.[4]

What does this mean? Technology will become more *available* and *more accessible* over time because we will be able to produce it faster and faster for less and less. Emergent technology that is expensive and largely unattainable right now will not always be that way. That's why it is wise to pay attention to emergent technology. As we prepare our students for their tomorrow and strive to incorporate technology into their educational experience, we are preparing them—and us—for the future.

My point in all this is not that technology is nearly impossible to define (even though it is). My point is that technology is always present, always changing, and often a bit challenging. But it's also tremendously helpful, once you get past the initial learning curve. As educators, we need to maintain an open mind toward technology in all its forms, knowing that eventually much of it will become second nature to us. I firmly believe educators are by nature innovators, and since technology is always intertwined with innovation, especially in recent years, we must be willing to face the learning curve with a sense of adventure.

To illustrate that point, let's take a quick look at a few technological advances in (relatively) recent educational history.

A Brief History of Technology in Education

Throughout history, educational institutions at every level have struggled with the effective and efficient uses of emergent technology. Many of the tools we use today initially generated heated debate and questions about their usage and management.

Take writing utensils, to begin. It took nearly one hundred years for the pencil (the original 1:1 device!) to be widely adopted in education, around 1900.[5] That means the pencil was once considered emergent technology.

Try to imagine the struggle and questions educators must have had when introducing the concept of using pencils in schools.

- Chalk and slate boards work just fine. Why change?
- They are used to chalk. How will we introduce this new tool to students?
- How can we control appropriate pencil usage?
- How can we keep pencils sharpened without disrupting class?
- What about the safety issues with sharpened writing devices?

Sound familiar? They are valid questions, and they should be asked: but aren't you glad a past generation was willing to see the advantages of "new technology," address the obstacles, and create a more positive learning environment?

While pencils continue to be a staple of educational supplies, the introduction of ballpoint pens in 1940 expanded students' writing options. Today, the variety and availability of media and colors accessible to students are unlike anything slate-and-chalkboard defenders could have imagined. And the digital stylus and other technology-based developments are pushing the horizon of writing even further.

Modernized writing utensils were only the beginning of innovation in education, of course. *Projection devices* have also experienced a rapid advance in technology. In 1870, technology included the Magic Lantern, a slide projector that projected images printed on glass plates. Next came the filmstrip projector, and then the overhead projector in 1930. The television eventually found its way into the classroom, especially after VHS players and tapes were introduced in 1977.[6] This teaching aid quickly grew into an exciting tool for classroom instruction. Today, modern projectors are commonplace, although they are starting to be replaced by 1:1 devices that allow video and other digital screen content to be displayed simultaneously across multiple devices.

Audio-based tools have also seen their share of advancement. Beginning in the 1920s, radio was seen as a revolutionary tool in classrooms. In 1932, Benjamin Darrow, founder of the Ohio School of the Air, was quoted as saying:

> The central and dominant aim of education by radio is to bring the world to the classroom, to make universally available the services of the finest teachers, the inspiration of the greatest leaders, and unfolding events which through the radio may come as a vibrant and challenging textbook of the air.[7]

It's worth mentioning that with the development of radios, education began to feel the pressure from outside forces that embraced newer,

trending technology. This societal love affair with technology would go on to include film, radio, television, and eventually computers. Parents and businesses in the 1920s supplied schools across the United States with radio receivers in an effort to integrate trending technology into their children's educational experience.[8]

Audio devices, just like other technology, have become exponentially smaller, cheaper, and more robust. Think of the impact of personal audio devices such as the Walkman and later the iPod and other MP3 players. Newer online services such as Spotify continue to revolutionize the audio reproduction scene and provide opportunities for creative learning.

With regard to *teaching tools* that allow us to reproduce and distribute teaching material, the invention of the photocopier in 1959 allowed for mass production of handouts, dittos, and worksheets. The impact the photocopier has had on education cannot be overestimated. Paper-based instructional strategies have become an essential part of the teaching experience, so much so that we now struggle with "going paperless." The next great shift in teaching tools involves an ever-growing array of online tools that involve less time, less waste, and far more options than photocopies.

Consider *calculation devices* as well. We've come a long way from the abacus and the slide rule! By 1975, there was one calculator for every nine Americans.[8] This new 1:1 technology was one of the first technology devices that pressed schools to provide access for all students and to seek to close a technology access gap. Because of the calculator, schools began to creatively approach funding to bring emergent technology into their classrooms.

Simultaneously, educators argued the pros and cons of adopting this emergent technology for achieving their curricular goals. Questions asked included:[9]

- How would calculators affect student computational skills?
- Would students become too reliant on machines?
- Would students be able to estimate?
- Would students learn from their mistakes?

With regard to *grading exams,* in 1972, the Scantron system—a scanner that could score a classroom set of quizzes in mere minutes—was introduced, allowing teachers to grade tests more quickly.[10] More recently, the availability of web-based quiz solutions has automated the process even further, freeing up valuable time to invest in students.

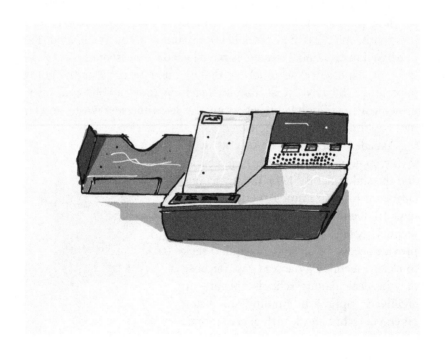

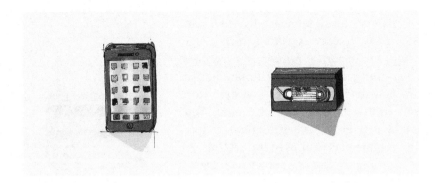

This brings us to the instructional uses of *mobile technology*. Probably more than any other development, mobile technology has revolutionized education. Relatively speaking, it is still in the early stages of adoption; but with the consistent decrease of mobile technology's cost and the increase in its reliability, mobile technology through cellular devices or cellular networks is the next emergent trend in learning.

This brief discussion is enough to note that with each new technology came new disruption of the status quo. But that disruption was temporary and—I think we'd all agree—well worth the effort it took to adapt.

The questions and arguments we have today about new technology in schools parallel the experience of our educational forefathers.

- What will students do with this new technology?
- How will students demonstrate learning?
- How can we control appropriate technology usage?
- How can we make it effective?
- Is this the best way for our students to learn?

What does history teach us about innovation, education, and technology? First, we learn *technology is not innovativeness*. From projectors to calculators to mobile technology, the only constant is that technology evolves and that educators agonize over how to use it. Let that ease your mind. In the history of education and technology, every educator at every level has asked the same questions you ask and has struggled with the same doubts you have. You are not alone in your uncertainty of technology.

History also teaches us that an *innovative teacher is willing to try new things and embrace failure as a learning opportunity.* Don't let the unfamiliarity of a new device, software, or system stop you from adapting and changing. You might struggle with learning a new app, but you are succeeding in innovating.

And finally, history shows us that educators always question what is best for their students, how to adopt new technologies, and how it could disrupt their classrooms. There is nothing wrong with questioning and nothing wrong with a little disruption in education. In fact, disruption often fosters the exact innovativeness we're looking for. We'll talk about that in the next section.

We can all agree technology is a good thing with great potential, and we can be tempted to rush to include new devices, theories, software, apps, games and more into our teaching. On the other hand, technology changes so fast it's hard to keep up. No matter how hard we try, we can feel we're being left behind by its rapid advances and even by our students themselves. We might fear we aren't up to the challenge of learning, using, and incorporating so much at once.

There is a happy, sustainable middle ground between those two sides. Rather than racing to embrace everything new just because it's new, we can evaluate what we are trying to accomplish and whether a particular innovative tool will serve us or distract us. And rather than feeling incompetent because we haven't mastered the latest apps or tools at our disposal, we need to give ourselves permission—and time—to learn. The learning curve can be overwhelming, but we don't have to achieve technology superstar status overnight. What matters is that we embark on the journey with wisdom, courage, and persistence.

I think of the earliest explorers of the world who were told the Earth was round. Scientists, cartographers, and great thinkers gave direction and contributed to the plans of these explorers, but not many of them went along to test their theory. That was up to the explorers. So is the educator's journey. We are told new innovations (technology or best practices) will work, but it's up to us to bravely go forth and apply what we learn. This growth can be highly disruptive to our *modus operandi* because it asks us to stretch far outside our comfort zone in order to increase our skills, but ultimately it leads to breakthrough and advance.

The Great Disrupter

Entire theoretical frameworks have been written to help us understand and address the reality that technology is the biggest disrupter of teacher experience. In other words, if you feel like technology (or the insistence of your school administration that you utilize certain technology) is constantly forcing you to rethink your teaching methods, you're not alone! I can't tell you how many times I've talked with educators whose resistance to innovation is based on one main factor: the amount of work it would take to implement that innovation.

I don't blame them. Teachers are always busy. But not making a little time now to learn a technology that will save you a lot of time in the long-term is inherently counterproductive. Or to put it more colloquially, you're shooting yourself in the foot. No one wants more work. But rather than asking, "How much time, energy, and stress is this new thing going to cause me up front?" you should ask, "How much time, energy, and stress will this save me over the long haul?" And if the answer is "Very little," maybe you should hold off on investing in that particular innovation for now. Just because it's shiny and new doesn't mean it's better. But if you're evaluating a technology or other innovation that is working for other teachers and has great potential for your classroom, look at the time spent now as an investment, not a waste.

One framework that addresses the disruption of technology in education was developed by Mishra and Koehler in 2006. They introduced a concept they call Technological Pedagogical Content

Knowledge (TPACK) as a way to conceptualize the need for teachers to adapt when teaching with emergent technology.[11] A teacher's TPACK is the result of the interrelationship of technology, pedagogy (our methods of teaching), and content (what we teach). If you have a chance, it's worth reading their detailed work and studying their analysis of the intersection and relationship between those three areas and how they affect education.

For the sake of this book, I'd like to simplify and apply the TPACK concept to the idea of innovation in education. I like to think of the intersection of these three things as the "teacher experience." I call it

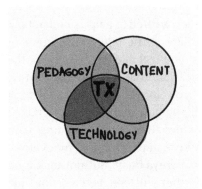

your TX. Your TX is your day-to-day practice and involvement as a teacher. It includes the material you teach, the various strategies and methods you employ to teach the material, and the technological tools you use in the process. Of these three things (content, pedagogy, and technology), what changes the most? And by extension, what causes the most disruption?

Let's think about each one, even though I'm sure you already know the answer. *Content* is relatively stable. Yes, teaching standards change from time to time, and new developments in science and other areas affect our teaching content. But overall, the changes are minimal and relatively easy to process as a teacher. If you take on a new class, you will be faced with a bit of a learning curve to grasp the material and the best way to organize it, but there are plenty of resources available to overcome that hurdle.

Pedagogy is also fairly stable. Again, teaching strategies change from time to time (which in itself is innovation). But those changes tend to happen slowly or to affect specific facets of teaching.

Before I move on to technology, let me point out that the stability of content and pedagogy mean that their own relationship (Mishra and Koehler call it PCK, or Pedagogical Content Knowledge) is typically quite stable. Navigating this pedagogy-content relationship is part of what every teacher does regularly. It simply means the teacher finds different ways to make the subject matter accessible to students. If our TX were defined just by content and pedagogy, it wouldn't shift much.

But everything changes when we introduce the third factor, *technology*. Why? Because it moves so fast, and it affects everything. There is nothing stable about technology. The only constant here is that there is no constant. No technology is absolute or guaranteed to last. And it shouldn't be—technology is about tools, and tools by definition exist to facilitate a process. If a better tool comes along, the older one will sooner or later become obsolete.

So what happens to our comfortable pedagogy-content relationship when we throw *technology* into the mix? The Venn diagram above looks like spinning plates, and that's exactly how teaching with new technology can feel! Adopting emergent technology causes massive shifts in our approach to both content and pedagogy.

Here's my point. Keeping a balanced pedagogy-content experience with rapidly shifting technology is the very nature of innovativeness. In other words, maintaining good teaching means constantly changing. We all want a stable teacher experience, but *stability* cannot be defined as static or stuck. Stability includes continually shifting, learning, changing, and rebalancing. It means learning to let new tools empower you rather than overwhelm you.

That's not easy, but it's also not impossible. And let me tell you from experience, it's worth it. You will find yourself facilitating student experiences and growth you would not have even considered possible just a few years ago. No one knows what shifts are just around the corner, but we know they are there. Our goal and responsibility are to integrate new technology knowledge with our existing content and pedagogy knowledge in order to maintain a balanced teacher experience.

Let the Games Begin

Even low-tech board games have levels of uncertainty. But just because we can't infallibly predict the outcome of a game doesn't prohibit us from strategizing for success. And who doesn't love playing games? The whole point is the uncertainty, the strategy, and the thrill.

The same principle is applied when we leverage innovation in our classrooms. The unpredictability of gameplay mirrors the constant changes we see in technology and innovation in general. No, we can't guarantee success. Quite the opposite—we can guarantee a few *failures* along the way. But that can't stop us from trying new things.

I'm using gaming as a metaphor for innovation, but I'm also a strong proponent of gaming in the classroom, for many of the same reasons. I think games provide a clear, relatable way for educators to model innovation, risk, and strategy for students.

Board games, card games, video games, and other forms of gameplay emphasize meaningful, experiential knowledge. Games illustrate the benefit of learning new things through firsthand experience. Even more importantly, they help us develop a fail-forward mentality, which is a skill set necessary for our learners to develop their own innovativeness.

Telling students to be resilient, to persevere, and to push through difficulties is not as effective as showing them how it's done. When they see adults fail, reassess, and problem-solve, they learn an invaluable lesson. Games allow us to model these behaviors and encourage students to practice them in a safe, non-threatening, fun environment.

Encouraging you to fail in front of your students may seem strange, but I assure you, it's a healthy experience. Too often we assume our authority depends on our perfection. Actually, in my experience, students respect teachers' honesty and authenticity more than their knowledge or skill. And I think they need to see us fail from time to time because they can relate more to our failures than to our strengths. For our learners to master grit in the face of adversity, they must observe it. They must learn it. They must practice it.

Games build a number of positive skills in students. According to one video game blogger,[12] the following skills are all learned through gaming.

Fortitude. Every gamer has felt a major upset, but once the despair falls away, it's the try-try-again attitude that defines a gamer. A true gamer can go from failure to failure without losing hope.

Dynamic. The mind of a gamer must be ready to change directions. New experiences lead to reworking strategies, modifying skills, and analyzing enemies.

Efficient. Gamers look for the most efficient way to pass a level. There will be risk involved in the exploration process, but it's a risk worth taking in order to improve. Worth noting: they rarely find the most efficient path the first time they play a level. Efficiency is the result of many attempts and many failures.

Empathetic. Many games require gamers to invest themselves into the character or protagonist. They are responsible for the outcome, so they are thoughtful about how they move forward.

Innovative. Gamers continually look for new experiences, new levels, new rewards, and new strategies. The entire gaming experience is about exploration and adventure.

Dexterous. Dexterity is more than just the ability to manipulate multiple buttons at the same time. It's the ability to multitask, to be flexible, and to quickly adapt.

Childish. Gamers understand that the process is meant to be fun.

Educating students in an increasingly Google-able world means shifting our fact-recall focus to experiential learning. Tangible, applicable learning experiences are necessary to support sustainable skills and knowledge for our students. Leveraging the engaging structure of simulations and games to achieve instructional goals can prove a powerful medium in experiential learning.

Experiential learning occurs when learning experiences are designed to foster context-based empathy. Empathy is defined as the action of being aware of, being sensitive to, and vicariously experiencing the feelings, thoughts, and experience of another. Teaching empathy is rapidly being recognized as paramount in preparing students for the world that awaits them.

For years I have led students on history-based simulations to colonize the New World, travel the Oregon Trail, and fight in the Civil War. The teachable moments in these experiences continue to be both widespread and poignant. Together, my students and I discuss our multiple perspectives of the same events, basing our discussions around their personal experiences during the game. I have observed many times how game-based learning can increase student empathy toward historical content. Through this emotional, empathetic connection, my students appreciate the experience of historical people, and that breathes life into our shared past.

Unfortunately, many educational games are not very engaging. There is one notable exception: *Oregon Trail*. Remember that game? Dysentery, cholera, broken wagon tongue...good times, right? Even the 1980s version of *Oregon Trail* excites students, although I use the 2001 version (OT v.5). If you are not familiar with the game, do a web search for it, and you are sure to find a version to play as well as bloggers romantically reflecting on their in-school gaming experiences.

When I was a middle school student playing Oregon Trail, I loved the hunting segments. The part about learning actual historical facts...not so much. So as a teacher, I redesigned this single-user game into a multi-user experience. The various tasks typically completed by a single player are divided up. Students are placed into groups and given directions specific to their tasks (trail guide, hunter, gatherer, trader, and so on). These groups vote on decisions pertaining to their task. This allows the entire class to be focused on one unifying event where all are involved. For three days, they compete against other classes for the much-coveted gold-star sticker award, tracking the progress of other classes on a National Geographic map posted publicly. During the days the games are in session, I find students running to class, rather than from it. Plus, the teachable moments are numerous. Collaboration, interdependence, consequences, critical thinking—monumental attributes can be illustrated from thoughtful gaming adoption and shared failure.

Games capture the attention of our students and are relevant to their world. Games appeal as an appropriate, approachable challenge that allows them to offer frequent feedback, leading to student satisfaction. If you are thinking of taking on a little more advanced gameplay like the example discussed here, I highly suggest user testing. Start a club or find some kids in a study hall and have them work out the kinks for you. They will love it, and you will have meaningful data to inform a full class rollout.

When employing gaming in the classroom, it is the job of the educator to relate and connect the activities to the required content. Admittedly, there have been times in my own classroom when I got caught up in the student excitement over gameplay and let the content-learning take care of itself—which it seldom does. But that doesn't mean I give up on games. I just figure out how to implement games in a more innovative and educational way.

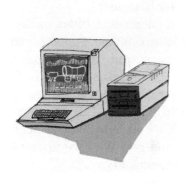

Regardless of whether you consider yourself a "gamer" or not, most of your students will have significant gaming experience. As we have seen, employing games (whether low-tech or high-tech) to engage learners will accomplish several key goals, including:

1. Modeling innovation
2. Modeling failure and resilience
3. Building empathy and firsthand (experiential) knowledge
4. Correlating learning and enjoyment
5. Unifying students around a common goal and shared experiences

I could list more benefits, but those are some of the main ones. It's been enough to convince me to rethink my teaching strategies and to continually be alert for ways to incorporate additional gameplay into my classroom. Let the games begin!

Make Tools Work for You

I mentioned above that the teacher's job with respect to games is to make sure the educational component is not lost. The same goes for all innovation, especially innovation that involves the use of technological tools. I've observed that much of our instructional practices today have been informed by tools, rather than good pedagogy guiding how the tools will be used. In other words, the tools are in control. (And if you've ever seen a movie where inanimate objects come to life and organize a rebellion, it never ends well for humans!)

If I could switch metaphors for a moment, I often think of technology as a ship and the educator as captain. A good captain commands his ship, not the other way around. The ship doesn't make decisions or sail on its own; the captain makes those calls. The ship can't navigate itself; it needs the captain to take charge and steer. He uses his tools, his knowledge of the sea, and his experiences to chart the best course. As educators, we have to act as captains, discovering which things will aid our journey. We have to captain the ship as opposed to letting the ship command us.

Let's take front-mounted boards, for example. Whether we are talking about the chalkboard, the whiteboard, or the smartboard, these front-of-the-classroom boards are designed to support the tea-cher's direct delivery of the content.

In doing this, however, we create a "front-row commodity" mindset. What is that? Do a quick web search for images using the keyword "teacher," and what you'll find are images of a traditional school experience in which the teacher is at the front of the class, always nearest the front row, with a chalkboard or other board in the background. Our societal norms teach us that the front row is where we find the board, and the teacher is anchored to the board; and therefore, the prime spot for learning is the front row. So what does that mean if you aren't in one of those coveted seats? No wonder parents want their children moved to the front row. And no wonder the back row is often associated with poor learning and poor behavior. Because the teaching tools are focused on teacher-centered learning, there is a benefit to being up close.

Of course, there is another way. There are many tools available that facilitate student-directed creativity and student-centered learning. In this scenarios, it doesn't matter where students sit, because their learning is empowered by tools, not restricted by them. For example, Chromebooks allow a teacher or student to share a file or screen to others around the room. Rather than ask everyone in a classroom to examine a painting being projected on the board in the front of the room, everyone can see it directly in front of them and investigate more closely. Through shared digital resources, students can work together to design and develop content-rich solutions that are paperless. Imagine not having to worry that a member of a group was absent during a critical component of the project, because through collaborative resources, ownership can be shared.

Technological advances such as laptops, tablets, and other 1:1 devices are better equipped to drive student-centered learning than many traditional teaching tools. That is one of the things that should most excite and motivate us to learn about new technology and other innovative teaching strategies. We have the opportunity to transform education and to put learning directly in front of students. We must allow technology to amplify our methods and to improve instructional practice rather than becoming the main focus of the learning. Use your tools; don't let them use you.

Culture of Innovativeness

It's important to remember that when it comes to innovation, you can't do it alone. Yes, you can make great improvements in your personal pedagogy on your own. But when it comes to the overall goal of educating our students, we need to create a *culture* of innovativeness in our schools. There shouldn't be just "that one teacher who is always trying crazy things"; rather, we should *all* we willing to attempt new things regularly. Schools should be a place where growth, innovation, and (reasonable) experimentation is fostered among teaching staff.

Our concerns about how, when, and why instructional technologies are being used are often symptoms of a greater problem in education: a lack of a culture that embraces innovativeness. As we've discussed, the word innovation refers to something new or to the process of improving an existing idea, product, field, or method. What if we were to think about schools as inventions in need of innovation?

A school culture that embraces innovativeness is a group of people who choose to frame their thinking around change. Not change for the sake of change, but change with a purpose, with direction, with intentionality. They recognize the need to dynamically approach innovation, usually in the form of tools and interventions, knowing they will never reach a place where they can rest on the laurels of past successes. This culture would not assume a static approach to teaching; rather, they would recognize that technology is dynamically changing, thus triggering consequent changes in how we function.

It is worth noting that simply integrating new technology will not change our practice or our paradigm. We need to think bigger than that and adopt a positive approach to innovation in general. As I said before, innovativeness itself is the pedagogy for the future.

The idea of innovativeness is both exciting and scary. It's a balance of cutting-edge applications of emergent technology and embracing failure as a necessary component to the learning process. Like any good journey, we grow and learn (often through a few wrong turns) as we become more capable travelers. Trying new things and falling in love with the process is an important mindset that will change our expectations toward the status quo. There can be no cruise control, no "this is the way we have always done it." The way we operate changes; therefore we are always changing.

The future of education will be shaped by our ability (as individuals and as a community) to meaningfully *adopt* innovation rather than forcefully *integrate* it. When a family adopts a new child, he or she becomes fully part of the family and is included in everything: family times, holidays, vacations, and even the inheritance. Adoption of an innovation implies more than just being tacked onto an existing culture: it implies acceptance.

Integration, on the other hand, denotes more of an obligation than a choice. It conjures up the idea of something that does not necessarily belong but was added on, like forcing a puzzle piece to fit even if it is from a different puzzle set.

Adoption of emergent technology is no small thing, but it is here we will find ourselves in a paradigm shift where learner-centered instruction will yield powerful experiential knowledge. This will produce increasingly tangible learning experiences for learners to connect with learning in ways previously not available through static, one-dimensional delivery. Further, learners will be afforded opportunities to leverage emergent technology to create authentic products for their individual learning context in educational organizations that embrace a culture of innovation.

For example, the future in our schools may see digital signage replacing student work taped to the walls. Where we once taught our students to write for local (peer or parent) audiences, we can now teach students how to publish content for a global audience. The learning curve has gotten so much easier in such a short time. It is not difficult to start a website, a podcast, or a YouTube channel. Students are already motivated by likes, views, and subscribers. So do we only begrudgingly integrate these new digital mediums into our teacher toolbox? Or can we choose adoption (i.e., shifting our practice and focus voluntarily and positively), and thus better prepare students for their future?

A Starting Point Checklist

Later we will take a more in-depth look at how individual educators can influence larger school culture, a dynamic that depends to some degree on the level of authority and influence a person has within his or her context. But to begin the conversation, there are several areas to note.

Author and researcher Don Ely has written extensively about the implementation of technological innovations in education. He identifies eight variables to consider in a school's culture when implementing innovation. I list them below, along with my own summary of each one. These conditions aren't meant to be an exhaustive list but rather a useful checklist of areas to evaluate and take into account.[13]

Dissatisfaction with the status quo. Typically, people don't see the need for change unless something is broken; so one of the first steps to change is feeling like there has to be a better way than the current state.

Existing knowledge and skills. A teacher must possess the competencies to teach students the use of these tools and help adopt emergent technology.

Available resources. The tools and relevant materials must be accessible to assist learners to acquire learning objectives.

Available time. Teachers need time to revise existing teaching plans, practice with new materials, and try out and evaluate new teaching procedures. This doesn't just include personal time but paid, in-service training.

Rewards or incentives exist for participants. If the current practice is going reasonably well, why risk new techniques? Why change? Teachers should be aware of rewards and incentives, whether intrinsic or extrinsic.

Participation is expected and encouraged. Individuals should be involved in decisions that will affect them. Participation may occur at many levels: during problem identification, consideration of alternative solutions, and decision-making about new programs or approaches to be adopted.

Commitment by those who are involved. Administrators should provide clear and visible support that endorses implementation.

Evident leadership: Leaders influence motivation by ensuring the necessary training is given and the materials to do the job are easily available. They are available for consultation when discouragement or failure occurs and continually communicate their enthusiasm for the work at hand.

Exploring these practical variables will allow us to better explain, predict, and account for the factors that impede or facilitate the adoption of innovation. I hope reading through this list inspires you to participate in your school's efforts to select and deploy meaningful innovation.

Waypoint #1

1. Emergent technology has had a profound impact on teaching. Think about the photocopier. What would your TX (teaching experience) be like without it?

2. The next time you make photocopies for your classroom, time how long it takes to make each copy, on average. Based on that, calculate the amount of time it takes to make a set of photocopies for a school day, then for a week, and finally for an entire school year—not even counting paper jams! Imagine not having to use the time and resources necessary to make photocopies. If you went paperless, how much time would you save a year?

Signpost #1: The Tools We Use

Tools are the methods and/or devices (technology) employed by teachers to teach.

1. What technology do you currently have access to in your classroom? Do you have a comprehensive list of resources available?

2. What tools would you like to have? Make a wish list.

Signpost #2: Rules We Follow

Rules refer to the regulations, norms, and conventions that constrain actions and interactions within our schools. Economically speaking, these are the financial opportunities and limitations that inform a school's activity process.

1. Do you know who/how to ask for items on your wish list?

2. The "digital divide" is the gap between those who have ready access to computers and the internet and those who do not. What steps are being taken to close the digital divide at your school?

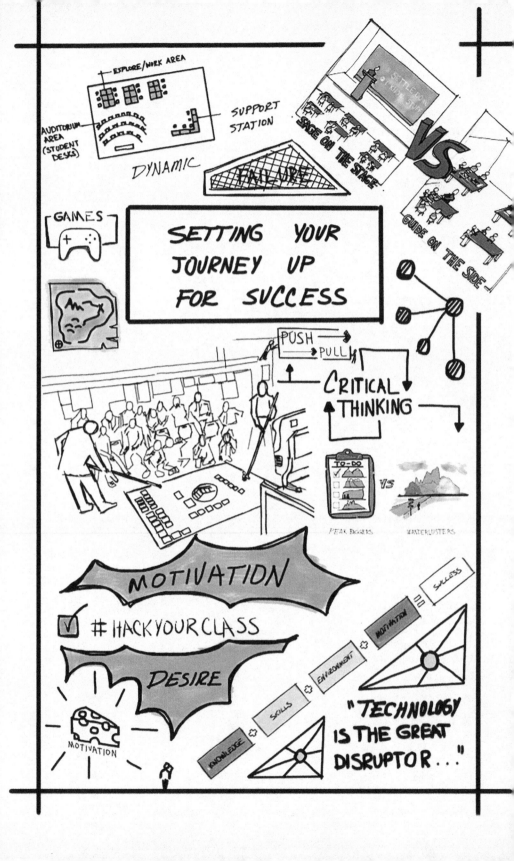

Setting Your Journey Up for Success

If you can imagine it, you can achieve it.
If you can dream it, you can become it.
—William Arthur Ward

In his book *Bugles* and a *Tiger: My Life in the Gurkhas,* ex-soldier and bestselling author John Masters describes his experiences in the British army in India during the 1930s. One of the stories he relates is a clear illustration of the inner innovation we need to succeed, even when the road we face is a bit uncertain:

A Gurkha rifleman escaped from a Japanese prison in south Burma and walked six hundred miles alone through the jungles to freedom. The journey took him five months, but he never asked the way and he never lost the way. For one thing he could not speak Burmese and for another he regarded all Burmese as traitors.

He used a map and when he reached India he showed it to the Intelligence officers, who wanted to know all about his odyssey. Marked in pencil were all the turns he had taken, all the roads and trail forks he has passed, all the rivers he had crossed. It had served him well, that map.

The Intelligence officers did not find it so useful. It was a street map of London.[14]

I suspect this Gurkha soldier was able to travel such an incredible distance through enemy territory not because he had a map that told him every twist and turn ahead (although he thought he did!), but because of his inner qualities of innovation, courage, and perseverance. He illustrates that what is most important in any journey is not *knowing* the future but being the kind of person who can face *any future* successfully.

We looked at innovativeness, which is the most essential element of our teaching journey, in the last chapter. In order to innovate effectively, however, we need to be intentional and comprehensive in our approach. It's like any journey: forgetting a couple of key items when you're packing (like your passport...or medicine...or underwear) can dramatically affect the quality of your trip.

I'd like to discuss four specific areas that require our attention. These are attributes that, if identified and fostered, will lead to a successful journey—even if you don't have a map. They are *knowledge, skills, environment,* and *motivation.* These four attributes were originally identified by Dr. Joe Harless, human performance technologist, in his "Performance Success Model." He used this model as a means to identify and intervene when people were underperforming.[15]

I often apply this model to the educational field not just to improve *performance* but to improve *innovation.* By examining our own knowledge, skills, environment, and motivation, we can equip ourselves to innovate successfully. Let's take a quick look at all four in the context of our wanderlust journey and then explore each one in detail.

Knowledge is the essential list of items we've brought with us on the journey, obtained through training and experience. *Skills* are picked up along the way through change and growth, like specialized gear we add to our packs as the need arises. *Environment* describes the conditions in which we embark and travel. *Motivation* is what drives us to continue, and it is directly connected to both our waypoints and endpoints (destination).

As you can see in the following Performance Success Model chart, the impact each attribute has on our journey is profound. If we are deficient in any one attribute, our teacher experience will be tinged with anxiety, frustration, feelings of being trapped, or apathy.

Performance Success Model

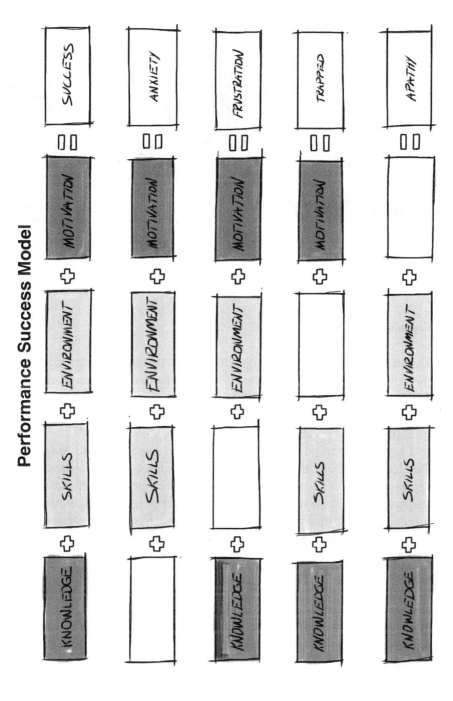

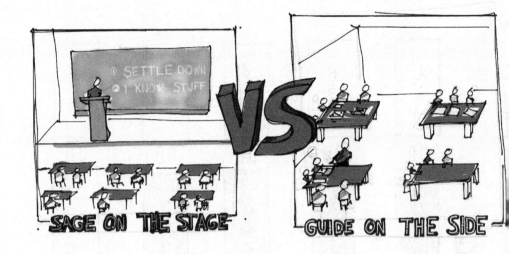

Knowledge

Traditionally, educators develop the bulk of their knowledge with the intent of being the "sage-on-the-stage," the one who knows the answers. Education, at least in the minds of many, is centered on a teacher who lectures, leads, informs, corrects, and controls, generally from the front of the class.

I say, "in the minds of many," though, because most of us know that lecturing from the front is only one aspect of our teaching experience, and often it's not the most important or effective. That is why we don't just study content: we also study pedagogy. Educational pedagogy is informed by psychology, which teaches us to understand the needs and motivations of our students.

Effective pedagogy is often more accurately described as being a "guide-on-the-side." Guides don't just recite information: they show people things and lead them to experience them firsthand. Roman emperor Julius Caesar is quoted as saying, "Experience is the teacher of all things,"[16] and a significant part of our roles as teachers is to lead students into a practical, observationally-based understanding of the subject matter.

It's an oversimplification, but the type of learning that comes from the sage-on-the-stage tends to focus on information, content, facts, and knowledge. The learning that comes from the guide-on-the-side includes facts but focuses more on the experiential learning of those facts, rather than memorization or mere mental understanding.

Both are important. I believe in the power of effective teacher-directed learning, and I believe in meaningful knowledge gained through experience. Each has a place in the classroom. So how do we leverage both? I think the key is to let each aspect inform the other. We've separated them here for the sake of understanding, but they actually work well together. Even when we are in the front, speaking to the entire class in a more traditional sage-on-the-stage format, we must remember the power of storytelling. Our approach might be content-focused, but it should still be wrapped in a story. We should show students why what we are saying matters. And when we are taking a backseat role to student-led learning and functioning more as guides, we should continually monitor and skillfully direct the content being communicated. We don't have to sacrifice learning to provide an engaging experience. Both are possible. Knowledge is naturally experiential; experiencing an engaging story and being coached one-on-one can both yield powerful results.

Skills

If I got an F the first time I tried to ride a bike, I wonder if I would have tried again? Luckily, I wasn't being graded at the time. I learned through failure, but I learned. And it's a skill that will serve me the rest of my life.

If knowledge refers to facts gained through learning and experience, skills refer to *abilities* gained through learning and experience. If we use the analogy of riding a bike, knowledge could include knowing what a bike looks like, watching videos of people riding bikes, and learning the theory behind riding a bike: pedal, balance, steer, brake. But while that is foundational and helpful to riding, it cannot replace the experience of actually riding a bike. Nothing takes the place of actually getting on the bike and learning what it feels like to pedal, balance, steer, and brake.

Riding a bike once isn't enough. Experiential application of skills leads to mastery; without the iterations, we will not learn the skill. We learn skills through repeated action.

Taking stock of the skills we need isn't the only important factor; we should also think about outdated skills we no longer need. For example, one skill I was particularly proud of was being able to clean the head on a VCR to maximize video quality. Clearly, some skills can be left behind.

That isn't to say everything that is outdated gets discarded. Sometimes our skills just need to be updated or improved. Apple doesn't start from scratch with each iPhone model, but rather builds upon the successes (and learns from the weaknesses) of preceding models.

To spotlight an educational example, we have learned multiple strategies for using video in the classroom. Whether it be VCR, DVD, or YouTube, we have learned that chunking video into smaller bits and having meaningful conversation about the content can make for more effective learning experiences. But can we build on this? Yes! From here we can leverage developments in video delivery to build off of our video skills and start using new features, like turning on subtitling to increase spelling and vocabulary retention. In this case, our pedagogy skills grow in an iterative fashion.

By assessing our skills, we discover the skills we need to add, the skills we have that are no longer useful, and the skills that if updated can serve us well. Another component to consider is where we gain or learn these skills. It can be humbling as an educator to recognize that our students might have more skills in some areas than we do, but let's face it—sometimes they do. I have found my students have a broad variety of skills with emergent technology that I can learn from while simultaneously helping them apply what they know more meaningfully. Accepting that others know more and that we can learn from them can save us a lot of time and trouble.

One day in study hall, my students saw me tinkering around on a PC. I had decided to upgrade the PC with a new DVD burner. I popped off the computer's casing and was preparing to install the new drive when a student said, "Hey, shouldn't you shut that off first?"

I quickly responded, a bit arrogantly, "I got this." I did not shut down the PC...and proceeded to fry the computer.

These moments of growth—to use a positive term—help us to not only rethink our skills but spot gaps where we need to improve and identify who could help us make those improvements.

Environment

Albert Einstein once said, "I never teach my pupils, I only attempt to provide the conditions in which they can learn."[17] Environment has far more to do with learning than we often realize. Research shows us that when learning occurs in a positive, safe, and affirming environment, our students will link new material with pleasant feelings so that the recall of information brings back a positive effect and produces more learning retention.[5]

At the same time, preparing an environment conducive to learning can be daunting. We have limitations in space, money, and time. That is why it's well worth the investment to look for creative solutions. Having a self-reflective assessment of the learning environment we have prepared for our students and understanding that it is an area for continual growth are very important. Try sitting in the back of your classroom and thinking of yourself as a learner in that space. From a student's standpoint, is it positive? Does your environment inspire?

When I first began doing this, I found much of my classroom setup was designed for me (the sage-on-the-stage) and not for my students. Thinking in terms of technology, my User Experience (UX) needed work. I needed a life hack, but for my learning space: a shortcut to efficiency and productivity. I started thinking of a few ways I could *hack my class*.

1. Classroom Mixtape

One hack I have found success with is music. What journey doesn't need a good mixtape? Music equals instant connectivity and attitude change in my students. Generally, there will be a positive emotional response and therefore a positive association with the classroom. I usually play a song-of-the-day in between classes as students exit and enter to engage them with the class space and set a positive environment.[18] Using music that is familiar to students tends to get the highest emotional response.

2. Seating Arrangement

The concept of hacking your classroom to develop inspiring spaces is something teachers have been doing for many years. We find ourselves with a limited space: four walls, usually one of those with windows, and twenty-five to thirty desks. And we are left thinking, *What am I supposed to do with this?*

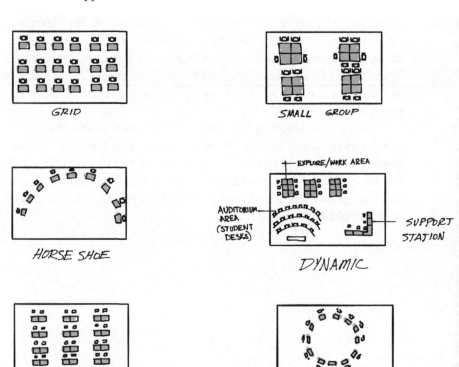

GRID

SMALL GROUP

HORSE SHOE

EXPLORE/WORK AREA

AUDITORIUM AREA (STUDENT DESKS)

SUPPORT STATION

DYNAMIC

PAIRS

CIRCLE

Most classroom chairs and desks are not nailed to the floor, and there is no ideal classroom layout for all instructional activities;[19,20] so move them around to try to find a match for you and your students. With a little ingenuity—and student input—we can create a space that inspires students instantly and can leverage their excitement for the remainder of the class.

In my seventh-grade social studies class, we were learning about the Puritans in New England, and I wanted to simulate the Puritan court. I changed the layout of my normal classroom to mimic a courtroom. I was struck by how engaged the students were by simply entering the room and seeing a different setup. The idea that students could come in and be excited just by a different atmosphere was something I hadn't really thought about until that moment.

For the remainder of the class, students were given jobs such as witnesses, defendants, magistrates, and bailiff. Student-centered tasks included writing the court notes on the board, standing and giving testimonies, and three magistrates passing verdicts (all guilty), complete with "appropriate" punishments. In each class, a student was banished to the hallway for heresy. I loved the looks on their faces as they were sent to the hall, all in fun.

3. Beautiful Accidents

Sometimes UX solutions are simple, even accidental. Be alert for that flash of inspiration that can come unexpectedly. When we first went 1:1 with Chromebooks in my school, I reorganized my classroom in the shape of a box with desks facing out so I could stand in the middle and see all the screens in the room.

I changed my room simply for classroom management's sake. What I found was that I had uncovered a huge projection screen— the floor.

This accidental discovery led to mounting a short-throw projector to an old computer cart so I could project onto the floor. My new "screen" is 7′ x 12′ and allows for lectures, gaming, and discussions in a new, engaging way; and it was all born out of trying something different in my environment.

4. Collaborate

Your classroom is not a fortress of solitude. Invite colleagues in and have a conversation about their best practices. (Teachers love a useful hack.) While you're at it, ask students for their ideas too! Do some research on inspiring spaces. Early in my career, a colleague came into my classroom and saw my desk, which was front-and-center and surrounded by bookshelves, and commented sarcastically: "Wow! That is quite a fort you have built." I had designed a bunker that truly illustrated the old "us vs. them" adage. Not the most welcoming of spaces! We must be prepared to say, "This just doesn't

work," or "This will do for now." Innovativeness is about change, so nothing has to be permanent. Instead of feeling trapped within the space you have been assigned, experiment with using it and other spaces to best benefit your learners.

Motivation

In our journey mindset, I like to think of motivation in terms of *peak bagging* vs. *wanderlusting*. Peak baggers are out to conquer one mountain after another. They have a checklist of things to get done in order to feel accomplished. They will sacrifice comfort and significant moments to collect check marks and victories. Peak baggers are extrinsically motivated, meaning they are motivated by external goals or endpoints.

Wanderlusters emphasize the joy of the journey. They explore with a deep desire to know more, and they are drawn to the discovery of new things. They are less interested in checking places off a list and more interested in experiencing the wonders of the journey. Wanderlusters are intrinsically motivated, meaning their goals are more internal than external.

In the field of education, extrinsic motivation can include salary, security, retirement, healthcare, and other benefits. These extrinsic motivators matter, of course; but how many of us got into teaching for the salary, security, retirement, and healthcare? I would argue that intrinsic motivation is really what drives us. It's what gives us a rich life experience.

I know this because, for many years, I was a peak bagger. A real one. I spent years hiking mountain peaks with friends, checking them off one by one, working to complete our lists. My strategy was to watch where I was going. Look down. Avoid tripping. Maximize my chances of success.

Looking back, I wish I had spent more time enjoying the view, seeing the beauty around me, and investing more in those friends who were on the adventure with me. One friend has since passed, and I cannot help but wonder: *If my focus had been less on peak bagging and more on wanderlusting, would I have been a better friend?*

So, should we just abandon our extrinsic focus? No—that's not what I'm saying. It would be a bit reckless to pretend our salary and benefits don't matter. Extrinsic motivations help get us going. We just have to be careful we don't pay so much attention to the checks on the checklist that we forget to look up, enjoy the view, and stay on course.

We all started our careers with a purpose and a plan but, as many of us know, things do not always go according to plan. It is in those times that we need to reflect on our intrinsic motivations and why we even started. Understanding why we do what we do can help us move forward in the hardest of times.

I had always viewed my tenure in public education as temporary, believing I would end up being a teacher-leader at the small school I attended as a child. After a decade of preparing and planning, I was offered the position—and then two weeks later, it was taken away and given to another person. It was a true heartbreak.

So what did I learn in this part of my journey? It wasn't to quit or give up on teaching (or I wouldn't be writing this book). In reflection, I realized I had literally been approaching every school year as my last. This, I have come to realize, was a real gift. I taught each year as if I had nothing to lose. I was able to devote my energy and time into my students then and there, with no concern about the next year, or about maintaining a long career by making people happy, or about a pension or retirement fund, or about a stable salary.

I did not realize at the time what a liberating experience this was. You might be thinking this sounds like some crazy, unrealistic approach to teaching; but let me define it for you with the tenets I have come to call "teaching with reckless abandon."

- Teach each day like it is your last. (Embrace the here and now.)
- Seek forgiveness, not permission. (Don't let our self-inflicted barriers prevent us from positively impacting our students' learning.)

Essentially, teaching with reckless abandon means to be your best today. Teach for now! This is a re-framing of our destination as 365 waypoints a year rather than one big retirement. I am hardly at the point in my life where I fist-pump with excitement every time my plans are destroyed, but I understand that sometimes the things that crush us can create building blocks for a more meaningful future. Honest reflection on where we have been can illuminate the path ahead.

One final thought: inspiration is reciprocal. In other words, inspiring others will inspire you. Sometimes when motivation—extrinsic or intrinsic—is lacking, you need to get outside your own head and give hope to someone else. It's amazing how quickly an investment in a student or fellow teacher can turn your own thoughts and emotions around.

In conclusion, these four attributes will help organize and guide your innovation journey. Remember to make sure you:

- Recognize how far you've come and how much still lies ahead (knowledge and skills).
- Understand the world around you and how to use it the best way possible (environment).
- Make it a practice to reflect on why you are on this journey and what truly matters (motivation).

Waypoint #2

Next time you have lunch with colleagues, try this for a conversation starter: "Tell me why you became a teacher." A rich, heart-to-heart conversation is sure to ensue (bring tissues).

To extend that conversation, compose a social media post where you articulate your reasons for becoming a teacher. This can be a brief, personal reflection; an anecdote or quote from a student; or a photo of a gift or letter you received from someone you influenced. If you have trouble keeping your word length down, write your thoughts out and share a screenshot or picture of the result.

Use the hashtag #whyiteach to join a beautiful conversation occurring internationally about why we chose this journey.

Signpost #3: The Object of Our Change

 Object: our objective is to innovate. As we move forward, we need to know how our school community embraces innovativeness. What strategies and/ or opportunities are in place that allow you to innovate in your school? List them below.

Who Are You?

Courage is contagious.
When a brave man takes a stand,
the spines of others are often stiffened.
—Billy Graham

Think about *Lord of the Rings*, *Harry Potter*, or *Star Wars*. Every good adventure story has a team of contributors, each with a special skill set that contributes to the team's success (and failures). They fumble about, illustrating the human experience, on their way to an epic victory. We are often engaged by both their plight and how we can relate to them.

A key character in these stories is the hero or champion. If you are reading this book, odds are, you are a champion, my friend. And if Queen is to be believed, you'll keep on fighting to the end...but I digress.

Champions

Many champions don't start off as champions in their story. They begin as regular people who stumble through the journey, feeling more like an imposter than an expert or leader. Perhaps it is this humble yet hungry and persistent drive that repeatedly pushes champions to keep learning and growing toward mastery. A champion is a perfect example of how mastery for the future is not found in a tool or workflow solution; it is found in innovativeness, in the champion's ability to change and adapt.

This willingness is extremely important because we can very easily assume the role of bystander in our school community. The bystander effect[21] is a scary aspect of the human experience that we must work against because it creates an environment of "not our problem" or "someone else will take care of it." This is a paralyzing condition that actively works against positive change in our schools. Champions are just the people we need to battle for that positive change.

Champions in the organizational adoption process are people who possess certain attributes and skills. They are transformational leaders who harness support from other members of the organization and can network well with colleagues. They are perceived as sensitive to colleagues' needs and are able to demonstrate an objective approach to finding meaningful solutions. They successfully guide projects through the approval hurdles, displaying persistence, expressing strong conviction in innovation, and involving key individuals.[22] They are the organizational mavericks who exist within a system but are given autonomy to explore alternative and creative solutions. An innovation champion must be tenacious, assertive, and decisive and should instill passion and positive thinking in the innovation process.[4]

In our journey to innovate, we can embrace this role for ourselves and/or find allies within the ranks. Selecting individuals who display these particular champion behaviors is undeniably crucial because an innovation is more likely to succeed if key individuals are willing to support the innovation.[23] Never underestimate the impact a champion has on both the adoption and sustainability of an innovation.

It's worth noting that champions come in all sizes, skill sets, and job titles. You might not see yourself as a maverick or adventurer, and you might not have a title or job description that puts you officially in charge. But you carry more weight and influence than you know. Culture change is by definition a collaborative effort, and we all have a part to play.

Types of Adopters

It is extremely important we recognize our strengths and weaknesses in our professional practice and know where we stand in the curve of adopting innovations, as illustrated in the chart below. You can take a personality test, a learning style inventory, or even a which-character-are-you quiz, but the power of meaningful self-perception is imperative. Such recognition can lead to real, positive growth.

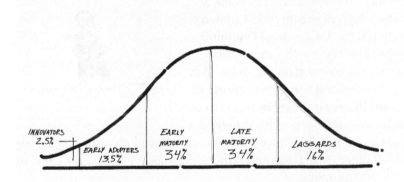

While you may take up the role of champion as a general way of perceiving your fit within your school system, you may find yourself identifying with another adopter category when discussing emergent technology. Adopter categories (innovators, early adopters, early majority, late majority, and laggards) can be illustrated on a bell curve on the basis of innovativeness, as illustrated in the chart above.[24] Read through the descriptions below and see where you fit.

Innovators: *"Let's do this!"*
Innovators are interested in new ideas from outside of the established local social system. Innovators do not have a map: they create a map. They forge ahead, accepting the consequences as they come. Innovators are generally able to understand and apply complex  technical knowledge. They are able to cope with a high degree of uncertainty about an innovation at the time of adoption. They learn from failure. Innovators are risk-takers and true adventurers.

Early Adopters: *"Describe the value in it and how to do it, and I am all in!"*
Early adopters are invested and res-pected in the local school community. Early adopters use the experiences of innovators to construct a map. They are cautious and want their efforts in-formed by research and best practices. Early adopters are not known for  risk-taking, but they have a reputation for well-thought-out execu-tion of emergent technology. Change agents seek this group out to speed up the adoption of innovation.

Early Majority: *"Show me my colleagues are using it, and I will try it too."*
The early majority adopts an in-novation just before the average person, making them an impor-tant link in a successful process  launch. They do not want to go first. They put weight on the impor-tance of curriculum and will proceed cautiously, using the early adopters' map to embark on their journey. They employ best practi-ces based on the experiences of innovators and early adopters.

Late Majority*: "I am a team player and I will support this, but I will probably not be the best at it."*

The late majority adopts just after the early majority. The late majority sees there is a map but is not sold on the purpose and is not really convinced this journey is for them. They adopt sometimes due to economic pressure, peer pressure, or both. The late majority must see the innovation as already being successful before they adopt. You might call them "team players" since they are willing to join the other adopters once they realize it is for the greater good. The late majority may not be very excited about technology of any kind, but they make the change for the benefit of their school community.

Laggards*: "I am not convinced this will benefit my classroom; I have done fine without it."*

Laggards like things the way they are—comfortable and predictable. They don't see a reason to change things when what they've always done works well enough. Laggards must be certain a new idea will not fail, see no other option, and/or be told they have no choice before they will adopt it. They are concerned about being blamed if the innovation fails to yield expected results.

Now that we've defined these adoption categories, there are several takeaways. Let's think about our own schools. First, these categories help us understand, as a whole, where our school culture stands. On the spectrum between innovators and laggards, where would your school fall?

Next, this model can be a predictor of how our colleagues may feel about adopting emergent technology, and it can help us identify where these colleagues stand. This will aid us in identifying early adopters, some of whom are likely respected champions in their circles.

To go a step further, by understanding these adoption categories, we better understand the sphere of influence each adopter carries. For example, an innovator can inspire early adopters and potentially some of the early majority, but he or she would be hard-pressed to motivate a laggard. Here's why. Innovators are often seen as people who do some out-there stuff, beyond the skill set or risk tolerance of later adopters. Innovators are, by definition, risk-takers. They accept the possibility of failure in a way that makes some people uncomfortable, especially those content in their comfort zone. Because of this, early adopters often serve as more effective connections in the onboarding process. They make up a larger percentage of people and have a reputation for a more measured approach to adoption.

Derek Sivers' Ted Talk called "The First Follower: Leadership Lessons from a Dancing Guy" illustrates the importance of early adopters in the adoption process.[25] (If you have not seen this three-minute video, please check it out.) Sivers uses different titles—leader and first follower—but for our purpose we will stick with innovators and early adopters. He explains that an innovator has the guts to stand out and be ridiculed, but that does not start a movement. The early adopters who join the innovator validate the movement (adoption) and make it appear less risky for others to follow. Then, late adopters model their behavior after the early adopter—not the innovator. Once the movement gains momentum, we see a real shift in cultural adoption. In this account, we must understand that the innovator treats the early adopter as a co-leader, an equal.

Decision-Making

If you are a decision-maker for a school or organization, there are multiple types of decisions which affect the adoption of the innovation process. These types might even be considered steps toward adopting innovation: (1) optional innovation decisions, (2) collective innovation decisions, and (3) authority innovation decisions.[26]

1. Optional innovation decisions: The choice to adopt or reject an innovation is made by an individual, independent of the decisions made by other members of the system. The individual's decision can be influenced by the norms of the system and by communication through interpersonal networks. An example of this may be a teacher from a school choosing to go paperless at their school while their colleagues continue to teach with paper.

2. Collective innovation decisions: The choice to adopt or reject an innovation is made by consensus among the members of a system. To keep with the paperless theme, an example of this may be a department level choosing to go paperless.

3. Authority innovation decision: The choice to adopt or reject an innovation is made by relatively few individuals in a system who possess power, high social status, or technical expertise. An example of this may be where upper-level leadership has decided their school community will go paperless, so they will no longer purchase printers or ink or service photocopiers.

As a leader, if you allow your innovators and early adopters the flexibility to make optional innovation decisions, their successes may naturally lead the early and late majority to a collective innovation decision. Finally, it may take the authoritative approach to move the laggards forward in the desired adoption.

Another thing to note is that a person's adopter category may (and probably will) change depending on the topic. An innovator in robotics may also be a laggard in the maker movement. An early adopter in virtual and augmented reality might be a late majority in mobile learning. There's nothing wrong with that. We all learn and grow at different speeds and in different ways.

In conclusion, remember that identifying the value of emergent technology within the context of our classroom is the first step toward becoming a change-agent in our professional communities. Change itself isn't the goal; it's the process. Once we realized the relevance of an innovation to our classroom, our approach and adoption category will reflect that. The same goes for those around us. Perceived relevance always informs adoption.

Once a specific innovation becomes a seamless part of our classroom, we have reached the pinnacle of innovative adoption. And it happens much quicker than you might think!

Waypoint #3

 After reading about the different types of adopters, you probably find yourself wondering, *what kind of adopter am I?* Take the short survey below to learn a little more about yourself.

Survey Instructions:

1. Thinking about your overall approach to innovation, compare all five words in each row and rank the words from 1 to 5.

> 1 = not me at all
> 2 = not very much like me
> 3 = sometimes like me
> 4 = often like me
> 5 = most like me

2. What did you think of the survey results?
How to interpret your results: Each group correlates to one of the five adopter categories referred to in this chapter. Read the description below to learn more about yourself and your approach toward innovation.

A	B	C	D	E	
Risk Taker	Logical	Calculating	Go with the flow	Reserved	
					RANK

F	G	H	I	J	
Intelligent	Dynamic	Content	Informed	Loyal	
					RANK

K	L	M	N	O	
Want Direction	Analyze	Take Action	Hesitant involvement	Support	
					RANK

P	Q	R	S	T	
Cooperative	Concerned	Flexible	Always Changing	Stable	
					RANK

U	V	W	X	Y	
Loner	Team Player	Cheerleader	Team Leader	MVP	
					RANK

Z	AA	BB	CC	DD	
Playful	Organized	Understanding	Devoted	Exploring	
					RANK

Add up all of your rankings for each group and add your totals

Group 1 (A, G, M, S, Y, Z)	Group 2 (B, F, L, R, X, DD)	Group 3 (C, I, O, Q, W, CC)	Group 4 (D, J, N, P, V, BB)	Group 5 (E, H, K, T, U, AA)

TOTALS:

61

Group 1: Innovators	Group 2: Early Adopters	Group 3: Early Majority	Group 4: Late Majority	Group 5: Laggards
Innovators are interested in new ideas from outside of the established local social system. Innovators do not have a map: they create it. They forge ahead, accepting the consequences as they come. Innovators are generally able to understand and apply complex technical knowledge. They are able to cope with a high degree of uncertainty about an innovation at the time of adoption. They learn from failure. Innovators are risk-takers and true adventurers.	Early adopters are invested and respected in the local school community. Early adopters use the experiences of innovators to construct a map. They are cautious and want their efforts informed by research and best practices. Early adopters are not known for risk-taking, but they have a reputation for well-thought-out execution of emergent technology. Change agents seek this group out to speed up the adoption of innovation.	The early majority adopts an innovation just before the average person, making them an important link in a successful process launch. They do not want to go first. They put weight on the importance of curriculum and will proceed cautiously, using the early adopters' map to embark on their journey. They employ best practices based on the experiences of innovators and early adopters.	The late majority adopts just after the early majority. The late majority sees there is a map but is not sold on the purpose and is not really convinced this journey is for them. They adopt sometimes due to economic pressure, peer pressure, or both. The late majority must see the innovation as already being successful before they adopt. You might call them "team players" since they are willing to join the other adopters once they realize it is for the greater good. The late majority may not be very excited about technology of any kind, but they make the change for the benefit of their school community.	Laggards like things the way they are—comfortable and predictable. They don't see a reason to change things when what they've always done works well enough. Laggards must be positively certain a new idea will not fail before they will adopt it. They are concerned about being blamed if the innovation fails to yield expected results.
Risk-Taker Dynamic Take Action Always Changing MVP Playful	Logical Intelligent Analyze Flexible Team Leader Exploring	Calculating Informed Support Concerned Cheerleader Devoted	Go with the Flow Loyal Hesitant Involvement Cooperative Team player Understanding	Reserved Content Want Direction Stable Loner Organized

3. But wait—there's more! Instead of completing this survey about your general adoption practices, try it again with a particular innovation in mind, and answer the same questions. Then see how your results compare to the first time you took it.

For example,
What kind of adopter are you when it comes to coding?
What kind of adopter are you when it comes to going paperless?

Signpost #4: Subjects

Subjects describe faculty and staff as adopters (innovators, early adopters, early majority, late majority, laggards). It is helpful to list who fits within these categories when framing our understanding about innovation.[27]

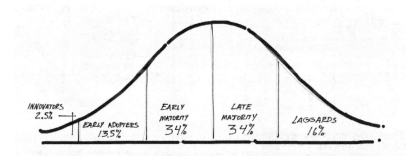

Select a few examples from your colleagues. Who do you think would belong in each category?

Innovators:
Early adopters:
Early majority:
Late majority:
Laggards:

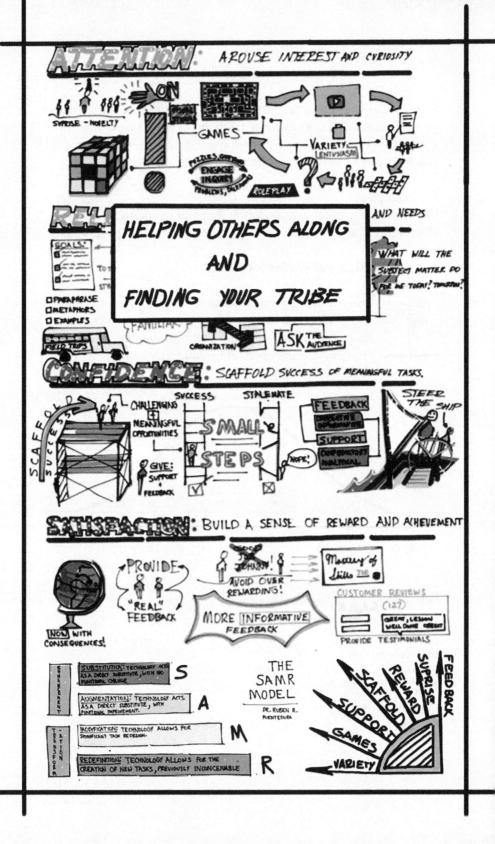

Helping Others Along and Finding Your Tribe

We awaken in others the same attitude
of mind we hold toward them.
—Elbert Hubbard

As a second-year teacher, I remember the excitement that ran through me about leading my students to participate in a certain project-based learning activity. I bolted down the hall with great enthusiasm to share my excitement with a veteran teacher I greatly respected. Unfortunately, the teacher's reaction was cold and even negative. He seemed offended I was trying a strategy he did not believe was worth the time it took. As I thought about it further, I realized this teacher would be the only one not using this new strategy, and perhaps he felt a loss of solidarity as I crossed over to "the dark side."

That encounter taught me a couple of things. First, I realized out-of-the-box thinking can be received in two ways: with fervor or hostility. Which one depends completely on the person we are sharing the new idea with. I realized the same goes for enthusiasm. While some colleagues find enthusiasm to be infectious, others perceive it as a threat.

Innovators and early adopters of emerging technology can often find themselves uniquely situated to help colleagues. And even if you are a later adopter, you will likely still find people around you who have yet to commit to innovative change and who would be willing to follow your lead. Often culture shift leaders do not have a title or formal authority to implement change—they simply have *success* in the innovation in question and *influence* with others who are more hesitant to adopt.

Maybe you've never seen yourself as a champion or a leader in the adoption of emergent technology or other innovations, but I think you should! You don't have to be a full-fledged techie or a crazy risk-taker to be a leader. As we saw in the last chapter, often it's the early adopters, rather than the innovators, who have the most influence. The real issue is this: there are people around you who can learn from *you*. They are watching you, they respect you, and they will follow you. Sometimes that "following" might be hesitant and accompanied by a fair amount of verbal negativity. But you are qualified and capable—and I might even say called—to help your colleagues become the best version of themselves. We are all on the same team, and we will all have those areas where, for whatever reason, we need someone to lead us by the hand. Be that person for those around you. Not only will you help them, you'll help yourself become a better teacher and peer leader.

How do we best help others understand the value of new technology and how it might benefit their students' lives (rather than just how it might fit into their classroom)? How do we ask colleagues to adopt technology they might not want to adopt without adding to their trepidation? And then, how do we help them learn that technology without putting our hands on their keyboard or their mouse and doing it for them?

The sage wisdom of the old proverb still applies: "Give a man a fish, and you feed him for a day. Teach a man to fish, and you feed him for a lifetime." This adage is very applicable to adopting emerging technology. We do not want to build robots but rather create innovators. We want to teach others how to receive new tools and adopt and value technology as *they* would use it—not as *we* would use it. This can be accomplished effectively through three strategies: vicarious experience, guide-on-the-side coaching, and the right frame of mind.

Vicarious experience: As champions (or those learning to be champions), it is part of our job to put ourselves in the shoes of late adopters or laggards to help them along. Empathetic understanding and real, meaningful relationships can promote adoption of innovation and inspire positive change.

Guide-on-the-side coaching: While we may be leading the adoption of innovation, we must take on the role of a guide. This means explaining to our colleagues where we are going, why we are going there, and what we hope to see when we arrive. Yes, it might be easier for us to have a see-things-my-way mentality, but that would not foster an innovative school culture. We are investing in others so they can pursue innovation independently of us.

Right frame of mind: We cannot approach supporting our colleagues with a judgmental mindset. (This often sounds something like, "Ugh. They are doing it wrong...*again!*") We must do our best to understand the context in which our colleagues operate, what motivates them to teach, and how we might serve them best. Rather than judging the level they are at, we help frame their unique skills and challenges and then guide them through exploring innovative ideas that support their specific situations.

ARCS Model

There are key stages we can use to measure and stimulate growth in the adoption of emergent technology and innovativeness in general. These stages can be summed up by John Keller's ARCS Model of Motivational Design Theories.[28] The ARCS model (an acronym which stands for Attention, Relevance, Confidence, and Satisfaction) is a comprehensive and very helpful summary of the key stages of motivating students toward learning. Keller's theory explains strategies and recommendations for improving educational effectiveness in a variety of classroom settings.

I'd like to apply these four stages not to motivating students but rather to motivating *educators* toward learning; specifically, toward innovating and adopting emergent technology and other "new" educational tools. Think of this as a process that starts with capturing their attention and moves toward the satisfaction they will feel when they realize, "I can do it."

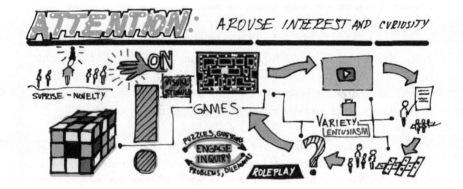

Attention

Before people see the relevance of using emergent technology in the classroom, they must stop and focus on how adoption is advantageous. That means capturing their attention with real-world uses and examples. It's often helpful to use a humorous anecdote or surprising fact. When I'm talking to people about a paperless classroom, for example, I'll often mention the number 42. No, it's not a reference to the *Hitchhiker's' Guide to the Galaxy*. It's the number of hours each year I no longer stand at the copy machine, making paper copies. That's an entire work week! And I'm not even figuring in paper jams or tracking down supplies.

Yes, a paperless classroom takes time and energy to begin, but like much emergent technology, it can increase workflow efficiency for both teachers and students. Time savings and workflow efficiency are highly important for educators, but they need to see it in action. Watching others perform new activities without adverse consequences can get their attention and change their perspective from feeling threatened to realizing that they, too, can improve if they persevere.

Finally, in this first step, take into account your delivery style and method. Newbies can easily conjure up fear-provoking thoughts about their ineptitude and can arouse themselves to elevated levels of anxiety that far exceed the fear experienced during the actual threatening situation. Take it easy; go slow.

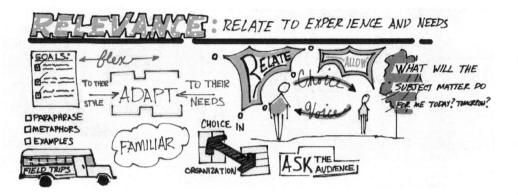

Relevance

For people to try new things and begin to adopt innovation, they first need to understand why it matters. Is there a need? A problem? From here, they can begin to frame their understanding around how it relates to their previous practice or how it builds off of something old or something familiar to them. Once that framework is established, the advantages—why this is beneficial to them—should be explained.

For example, VCR and VHS tapes allowed us to record, play, fast-forward, and rewind, but the tape was not usable after many showings and sometimes the tape ripped. Likewise, DVDs allowed us to record, play, fast-forward, and rewind, but the digital quality was much better and remained constant—unless you scratched the DVD. YouTube videos can be recorded, saved, added to a playlist, played, fast-forwarded, and rewound, and they do not lose their quality. Thus by framing YouTube around our past adoption of VHS tapes and DVDs, we can see the advantages and benefits of using it.

When we take the time to persuade our colleagues about relevance and why adopting innovation matters, they are likely to mobilize greater effort than those who are not persuaded (but rather told).

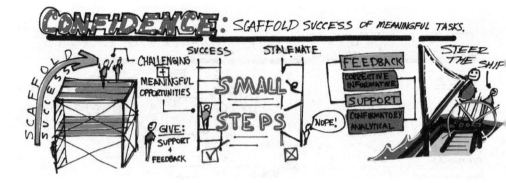

Confidence

Emergent technology can be fairly complex on its own. Add to that being told that things are going to change every six to eighteen months.[29] That can feel pretty overwhelming to those who have yet to embrace innovativeness. To assist colleagues, we need to establish a "try everything" environment where they feel comfortable aiming high, knowing that even if they fail in front of you, they are safe and supported. Michelangelo is quoted as saying, "The greatest danger for most of us is not that our aim is too high and we miss it, but that it is too low and we reach it."[30]

Baby steps are key here. If they feel they can't succeed, they are more likely to give up. Leveling the difficulty of the task will allow for early successes, keeping them motivated and yielding increased attempts at more difficult tasks later on. This will eventually and naturally lead to the decision to adopt. We know failure is the greatest teacher, yet we are still afraid of it; however, through productive struggle and support, colleagues will learn to personally master experiences with something new.

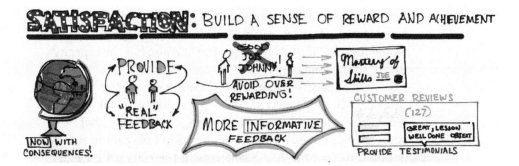

Satisfaction

Satisfaction refers to the idea that learning should be rewarding to the learner. There should be internal satisfaction or external rewards linked to the learning process. For teachers, this satisfaction is usually directly correlated to their time, efficiency, and effectiveness in the teaching role.

Since emergent technology and other innovations exist to improve teachers' toolboxes, as soon as they see results from their efforts, they begin to feel the satisfaction they need to continue. Satisfaction resides in the willingness of the teachers to adopt the technology and apply it to their professional settings. Your role as champion is to help them advance toward adoption and to see those benefits.

It's helpful to set teachers up for small wins rather than shooting for an impossible goal. Let them see how incremental steps reduce their workload, engage their students, expand their teaching possibilities, and in general make them better teachers. They will then be internally motivated to tackle greater innovation challenges.

Application of these four attributes can be found in many different industries. An article in the *Harvard Business Review* on employee innovation states that if employers want their employees to be more creative in their day-to-day work, they can't rely on Ping-Pong tables, bean bag chairs, or one-off events like hackathons. To encourage more innovation and foster a sense of challenge, they should:

- Give employees projects that are demanding, while also making sure the tasks are a good match for their skills and resources.

- Don't just give a new project to whoever has free time or could finish it most easily. Before delegating, ask, "Who would feel challenged by this project and also has the capacity to rise to the challenge?"
- Aim for 70% success. If employers expect everyone to complete a task with 100% success, they are unlikely to take risks, which is an innovation killer. Letting them know that 70% success is acceptable will ensure they don't play it too safe.[31]

It's not hard to spot the ARCS concepts in the Harvard Business Review article. Appropriately demanding tasks get people's attention, jobs that are a good match for skills and resources speak of relevance, appropriately challenging work is a requirement for confidence, and expectations for reasonable success rates produce satisfaction.

These attributes apply to business, the classroom, and our professional development opportunities. It's just plain common sense. When we learn to employ smart motivational models to our innovation journey, there's no limit to what we can accomplish.

Teacher Efficacy

At its core, the ARCS model is about the motivational design of instruction, which refers to the influences on our desire to learn. While motivating someone who doesn't want to be motivated is nearly impossible, it is possible to create conditions that will spark their interest and set them up for success. From there, it's up to them; but I will say—success breeds serious motivation. If they get a taste for achievement (the satisfaction we talked about above), half the battle is won.

Authors Megan Tschannen-Moran and Anita Hoy have done fascinating research on "teacher efficacy belief," which refers to teachers' judgment of their capabilities to bring about desired outcomes of student engagement and learning. They show that efficacy is related to how teachers make decisions, shape goals, implement planning and organization, react in the classroom, and relate to students. In addition, teachers with high self-efficacy embrace new ideas and methods for teaching.[32]

In other words, attitude matters. Belief in yourself matters. Psychologist Albert Bandura says the strength of people's convictions in their own effectiveness is likely to affect whether they will even try to cope with given situations.[33] And Everett Rogers is even more specific when he concludes that in developing a favorable or unfavorable attitude toward an innovation, people may mentally apply the new idea to their present or anticipated future situation before deciding whether or not to try it.[34]

In my experience, people tend to write ideas off too quickly, often doing so because they write *themselves* off too quickly. They look at their circumstances, at themselves, and at the proposed innovation, and they make a value judgment about whether they are likely to succeed. Often, because of past mistakes or because they are afraid of future mistakes, they opt not to take the risk.

That is where you as champion, coach, or cheerleader (pick your favorite metaphor), come alongside to encourage people through the process. Get their attention, show relevance, build their confidence, and celebrate their satisfaction with them when they've taken a risk and succeeded. Their success builds self-efficacy, meaning the next challenge won't be so challenging. Eventually, people who are initially resistant often develop innovativeness and become champions themselves.

SAMR Model

Another powerful model that sparks discussion with colleagues regarding technology adoption and pedagogical-shift strategies is Dr. Puentedura's SAMR model.[35] SAMR is a framework to measure the impact of technology or digital tools. However, the model doesn't focus on improving the *tool* itself but instead aims to measure the improvement of the *goal* you are attempting to achieve through using the tool. This tool can be used for individual reflection and improvement, but it is especially helpful when it becomes part of a larger discussion connected to improving a culture of technology adoption across a wider area, such as a department or entire school.

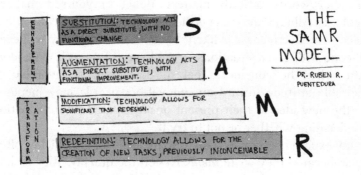

Substitution. This refers to replacing an existing teaching strategy or activity for one that is supported by emergent technology.

Augmentation. This means building upon our original strategy by finding ways technology can improve (rather than simply replace) the strategy.

Modification. The next level is to use technology to redesign the strategy significantly.

Redefinition. Technology allows us to not just edit or improve the strategy, but to create a new strategy beyond what we could ever have accomplished without the technology.

The SAMR model helps us to rethink individual lessons, units, and instructional practice. For example, we can take a paper worksheet packet, make it digital (substitution), then use digital tools to annotate it (augmentation), then redesign the activity to include a slide deck or video (modification), and finally create a completely new activity that accomplishes the original activity's purpose but more effectively (redefinition). For various teacher and student tasks, a SAMR evaluation might look like these examples:[36]

TEACHER APPLICATION: SAMR Model

Class Task	Substitution: A direct substitute, with no functional change	Augmentation: A direct substitute, WITH functional improvement	Modification: Significant task redesign	Redefinition: Creation of new tasks, previously inconceivable
Handouts - File Sharing	Send class materials as attachment	Share link to files	Create a website with files linked	Online classroom
Distributed Readings	Provide students with a PDF	Insert text boxes on PDFs to complete tasks	Use text-to-speech applications with PDF annotator	Students record themselves reading and reviewing using screen recording
Assessments	Online quiz	Online quiz with auto-grading	Online quiz with auto-feedback for incorrect questions	Students complete assessment option of their choice and upload it to the online classroom

STUDENT APPLICATION: SAMR Model

Class Task	Substitution: A direct substitute, with no functional change	Augmentation: A direct substitute, WITH functional improvement	Modification: Significant task redesign	Redefinition: Creation of new tasks, previously inconceivable
Note taking	Take notes in a digital document	Take notes with a cloud-based document	Create document with hypertext for notes	Collaborative notes
Research	Copy and paste content from websites	Bookmark and summarize information with a cloud based tool	Use web browser tools to record sources	Student creates workflow process
Presentations	Make a digital slide-based presentation	Create a collaborative, slide-based presentation with another student	Use online resources to bring in content and to format slides	With presentation tools: take audience questions while presenting

Finding Your Tribe

As we think beyond working with one colleague at a time, we must begin to think about developing our culture. If you are alone on your journey to innovate, you're doing it wrong! You need to find your tribe, those people who share your passions and abilities. This includes your Professional Learning Network (PLN) which is typically worldwide. Your PLN is your tribe. It is made up of like-minded people you have developed a network with. Your PLN is totally customizable. Your PLN is a place where unconventional ideas and out-of-the-box practice can come to fruition. Your challenge is to *grow* this community. Social media provides us with a meeting place to have both asynchronous and synchronous conversations about our instructional practice, our interests, and our students' future.

Your Professional Learning Community (PLC), on the other hand, is local and consists of the educators around you. Your PLC seeks to navigate existing structures to meet learner goals. Your challenge is to *communicate* with this community. Major attributes of PLCs include the following:[37]

- **Supportive and Shared Learning:** the facilitative participation of administrators who share leadership and authority by inviting staff input in decision making.
- **Collective Learning:** application of collective learning to address student needs.
- **Shared Values and Vision:** a shared vision that is developed from the teachers' commitment to student learning.
- **Supportive Conditions:** time scheduled for teachers to come together to learn, make decisions, problem solve, and create work exemplified by collaboration.
- **Shared Personal Practice:** a peers-helping-peers process, based on a desire for individual and community improvement along with mutual respect and trustworthiness of the teachers involved.

These five major attributes are reflective of Albert Bandura's emphasis on performance accomplishment, vicarious experience, verbal persuasion, and emotional arousal.[38] *Performance accomplishment* means that seeing others succeed raises mastery expectations for yourself. *Vicarious experience* means that seeing others perform threatening activities without adverse consequences can generate expectations in observers that they too will improve if they intensify and persist in their efforts. *Verbal persuasion* means we can be socially persuaded that we possess the capabilities to master difficult situations by viewing other people attempting the same task. Finally, *emotional arousal* means we focus on the positive, on our ability to succeed, rather than allowing fear-provoking thoughts about our ineptitude to elevate anxiety unrealistically.[39] The research shows themes in community building and job satisfaction for teaching professionals.

The best practices found in effective PLCs can help significantly. PLCs can have multiple levels and contexts (team of teachers, building staff, school district of teachers, group of common content teachers, and more), yet the focus of every PLC must be to explore three major questions:

1. What do we want each student to learn?
2. How will we know when each student has learned it?
3. How will we respond when a student experiences difficulty in learning?[40]

Contextualizing these conversations around innovation and addressing gaps in connection for students yields positive change. Giving voice to our travel companions will tighten our bonds, strengthen our resolve, and bring us through the most difficult parts of our journey.

Social Connectedness

As I stated at the beginning of this section, this isn't a profession you should go at alone. In an effort to understand why teachers continue to teach in a challenging career, I once conducted a survey of seventy-five middle school teachers, asking them to identify why they stayed in their profession.[41] I was looking for attributes that teachers perceived led to their success and why they stayed in the educational field. What I found was many of them valued relationships with their colleagues more than most other outside factors.

These findings are parallel with teachers who were identified in a federal study on teacher mobility as *movers* (teachers likely to move to another school) or *leavers* (teachers likely to leave after their first year). These teachers described teaching in isolation as one factor that contributed to teacher dissatisfaction. Teachers identified as *movers* left the schools where they worked in isolation for schools where colleagues interacted and shared ideas.[42]

On the contrary, studies on the impact of colleague support and teacher retention also found that beginning teachers who were provided a common planning time and a scheduled time to interact and collaborate with colleagues were 25% less likely to move and 42% less likely to leave after their first year.[43] Those teachers, titled "settled stayers," described their supportive colleagues as a reason for their decision to stay at their school.[44]

Through my own experiences working with schools, I have found that directors of technology and key decision-makers seeking to roll out emerging technology find a great deal of success when they have positive relationships with their colleagues and with their employees. Our social connectedness is very important.

How do we leverage social connectedness with colleagues who have a bit of difficulty adopting new technologies? Here are two main ways.

Mentoring Programs

Effective and efficient mentoring should offer deliberate psychological and professional development conditions necessary for the development of teacher knowledge, skills, and dispositions, thus increasing teacher retention. It is a professional role that requires professional renewal, enhanced self-esteem, more reflective practice, and leadership skills. The knowledge and skills that experienced teachers acquire as part of mentor training and practice is continual professional growth.[45]

Sometimes mentoring can be framed more as peer coaching. The term *mentoring* infers that someone is new to a program or profession and is being guided to learn the craft. *Coaching*, on the other hand, refers to providing growth to an experienced person or audience who is learning a new skill or needs help filling gaps in practice. When mentoring is viewed as peer coaching, and when teachers plan, demonstrate, and practice new instructional practices in a collaborative manner, schools may find less teacher isolation and fragmentation, which as we learned, lessens the likelihood of leaving.[46]

Professional Development

Professional development (PD) is another way we can support teachers in a social-connectedness style. Professional development in education is responsible to promote teacher growth in a valid and practical manner. A community of teacher-learners can effectively promote this growth beyond what in-servicing alone can accomplish. Workshops and other in-service events are magnified by collaborative, shared-experiences. As teaching professionals, we *need* to learn, share, and collaborate with our peers to feel successful and believe in our ability to succeed.

Professional development offerings can be the catalyst for positive change. We have spent a great deal of time in this book discussing adopters and who we are in the story. Understanding ourselves and our colleagues can yield context-based, empathetically considerate, professional development opportunities. A combination of the ARCS model and SAMR model is an excellent strategy for creating professional development offerings, as we'll see below.

Teaching can be a lonely profession, often with a close-my-door-and-teach mentality. We are surrounded by people at school, but when the bell rings in our classrooms—it's just us. It is easy to find yourself feeling detached and alone. Yet, there is a wealth of knowledge and experience that can be accessed through well-structured collaboration opportunities, including mentoring and professional development. It will take effort on the part of the teachers, administrators, and institutions of learning, but the effort *will* generate positive results because the reciprocal nature of inspiration is that inspiring others will inspire you.

ARCS Workshop Exercise

Designing effective and efficient professional development offerings may be exactly what you need to do to help others along. Create your own PD workshop that employs the ARCS model to motivate and inspire your attendees. Use the following outline to brainstorm a workshop that leverages collaboration and social connectedness to inspire innovation in your colleagues.

A) Attention: arouse interest and curiosity.
  1. Description
      • Stimulate perceptions (surprise, uncertainty, novelty, juxtapositions).
      • Engage inquiry (puzzles, questions, problems, dilemmas).
      • Create variety (different kinds of examples, models, exercises, and presentation modalities).
  2. Examples
      • Incongruity; conflict
      • Games; roleplay
      • Hands-on/minds-on methods
      • Questions; problems; brainstorming
      • Videos; mini-discussion groups; lectures; visual stimuli; storytelling
  3. Reflection: How does an instructional leader's enthusiasm change attention?

B) Relevance: relate to experience and needs.
  1. Description
      • Allow audience to select or define goals; give examples of goals; discuss value of goals.
      • Adapt to what the audience wants to cover or how to cover it.
      • Use familiar communication modalities; relate goals to something familiar such as prior knowledge or experiences.
  2. Examples
      • Paraphrase content; use metaphors; give examples.

- Ask audience to give examples from their own experiences.
- Give audience choice in how to organize what they learn; explain how the new learning will use students' existing skills.
- Explain or show: "What will the subject matter do for me today? Tomorrow?"

3. Reflection: How do teaching models, field trips, portfolios, and student choice change relevance?

C. Confidence: scaffold success of meaningful tasks.

1. Description

- Set clear goals, standards, requirements, and evaluative criteria.
- Give challenging and meaningful opportunities for successful achievement within available time, resources, and effort.
- Encourage personal control; show or explain how effort determines success (personal responsibility equals achievement).

2. Examples

- Allow audience to choose goals.
- Allow small steps for achievement.
- Give feedback and support.
- Provide learners with some degree of control over their learning and assessment.
- Show that success is a direct result of personal effort.
- Give confirmatory-corrective-informative-analytical feedback rather than social praise.

3. Reflection: How do clear organization and easy-to-use materials change expectations for success?

D. Satisfaction: build a sense of reward and achievement.

1. Description

- Support learning applied in real-world or simulated context with consequences.

- Provide feedback after practice to confirm, analyze, or correct performance.
- Apply consistent consequences for meeting standard-consistent evaluation criteria.

2. Examples
- Avoid over-rewarding easy tasks.
- Give more informative feedback rather than praise or entertainment value.
- Use practical examples related to audience interests; award certificates for mastery of skills.
- Provide testimonials from previous audience about value of the learning.
- Give evaluative feedback using equitable criteria.

3. Reflection: Why does social praise not work as well as informative feedback in creating satisfaction? How do rubrics change satisfaction?

Waypoint #4

Walk through the SAMR model with a real example. Start with a simple paper-based lesson, perhaps a worksheet activity. How can you move it through this chart?

My paper-based lesson is:

Substitution: how can I make this activity digital (pdf)?

Augmentation: how can I improve the efficiency of this lesson with digital annotating tools?

Modification: how can I move past pdf and achieve the same content goals with effective tools?

Redefinition: if money were no object, what could I do with my students to support their understanding?

In the Redefinition stage, planning with a money-is-no-object mindset is appropriate. As we explored, the cost of new technologies decreases over time. We should start planning for a future with access to what we need.

Signpost #5: Subject 2.0

Professional Learning Communities (PLCs) and Professional Learning Networks (PLNs) are powerful for creating and sustaining positive change.

My PLC

List the top five PLC members you most interact with. I suggest listing those you interact with face-to-face.

My PLN

Next, list your top five PLN contributors. These are of your own making. Your PLN is custom-crafted by you and often comes through some sort of social media.

Dynamic Equilibrium and Other Culture Goals

A person susceptible to "wanderlust" is not so much addicted to
movement as committed to transformation.
—Pico Iyer

As we have seen again and again, the best journeys are not taken alone; they are full of rich relationships. Together we go through the highs and lows of life, forming our own understandings, our own inside jokes, our own views of our profession—our own culture.

Culture is defined as the beliefs, social forms, and material traits of a social group. Historically, cultures have been formed through one great catalyst: geography (i.e., physical proximity). These groups, connected by time and location, make sense of their world together; shaping a set of shared attitudes, values, goals, and practices that characterize them as a group or organization.

Today, we live in an age where time and distance do not bar us from engaging and connecting; however, our contacts and our local geography continue to be important during the process of adapting our practices. Our school cultures must provide a voice to all who are impacted by impending change. When we allow our decision-making to be driven by outside influences, rather than those invested in our direct community, we are setting ourselves up for consequences that we often cannot anticipate.

The following story of the Yir Yoront tribe in Australia illustrates the unintended consequences that can occur when we make decisions without fully taking into account our local context. It is based on an analysis originally conducted by Lauriston Sharp, the Goldwin Smith Professor of Anthropology and Asian Studies at Cornell University, and summarized by Edward Spicer in "Human Problems in Technological Change" and later by Rogers in *Diffusion of Innovation.* I am including it here in its entirety to illustrate the importance of wise, context-based innovation.

Not Just an Ax

The consequences of the adoption of steel axes by a tribe of Australian aborigines vividly illustrates the need for consideration of the undesirable, indirect, and unanticipated consequences of an innovation. The Yir Yoront traveled in small nomadic groups over a vast territory in search of game and other food. The central tool in their culture was the stone ax, which the Yir Yoront found indispensable in producing food, constructing shelter, and heating their homes. A complete revolution was precipitated by the replacement of the stone ax by the steel ax.

Anthropologist Lauriston Sharp (1952) conducted his investigation of the Yir Yoront by the method of participant observation. He studied Yir Yoront culture by taking part in its everyday activities. Because of their isolation, the tribe was relatively unaffected by Western civilization until the establishment of a nearby missionary post. The missionaries distributed many steel axes among the Yir Yoront as gifts and as payment for work performed.

Previously, the stone ax had been a symbol of masculinity and of respect for elders. Only men owned stone axes, although women and children were the principal users of these tools. Axes were borrowed from fathers, husbands, or uncles according to a system of social relationships prescribed by custom. The Yir Yoront obtained their stone ax heads in exchange for spears through bartering with other tribes, a process that took place as part of elaborate rituals at seasonal fiestas.

When the missionaries distributed the steel axes to the Yir Yoront, they hoped that a rapid improvement in living conditions would result. There was no important resistance to using the steel axes, because the tribe was accustomed to securing their tools through trade. Steel axes were more efficient for most tasks, and the stone axes rapidly disappeared among the Yir Yoront.

But the steel ax contributed little to social progress; to the disappointment of the missionaries, the Yir Yoront used their new-found leisure time for sleep, "an act they had thoroughly mastered." The missionaries distributed the steel axes equally to men, women, and children. Young men were more likely to adopt the new tools than were the elders, who did not trust the missionaries. The result was a disruption of status relations among the Yir Yoront and a revolutionary confusion of age and sex roles. Elders, once highly respected, now became dependent upon women and younger men, and were often forced to borrow steel axes from these social inferiors.

The trading rituals of the tribe also became disorganized. Friendship ties among traders broke down, and interest declined in the annual fiestas, where the barter of stone axes for spears had formerly taken place. The religious system and social organization of the Yir Yoront became disorganized as a result of the tribe's inability to adjust to the innovation. The men began prostituting their daughters and wives in exchange for the use of someone else's steel ax.

Many of the consequences of the innovation among the Yir Yoront were undesirable, indirect, and unanticipated; these three types of consequence often go together, just as desirable, direct, and anticipated consequences are often associated.[47]

Beware Assumptions

What do we learn from the Yir Yoront story? The unintended consequences of adopting innovation will vary within each culture. Assuming innovation will benefit one culture because of another culture's success is dangerous. This assumption has led to countless other problems in history.

During my graduate coursework, I observed the increasing prevalence of laptops in instructional spaces. (I know—that dates me.) Laptops are a very powerful tool which can, of course, be leveraged for meaningful learning. But I saw at least half of my peers barricaded behind open screens for most of the class during lecture. I found myself wondering, *What are they typing? What are they looking at? Are they just checking social media?* Their eyes down and the clickety-clack of the keyboards must have had an effect on instructors.

This was eye-opening for me. It was a chance to be the learner and think about my impact on the instructor, which directly led to a pedagogy shift in my classroom practice. As a classroom teacher, I now tell my students to "listen with their eyes" and, when using laptops, to "lower" or "pizza box" their screens during direct instruction.

Over the past two decades (our Digital Age), we have seen ourselves accepting certain classroom-space barriers as acceptable. The stationary desktop computer as a source of learning has shifted to laptop computing, where the learning has become mobile and asynchronous. Yet in a classroom setting, these useful technologies can create a social barrier, separating the learner from the learning and separating the content expert from the class with the flip up of a physical screen.

Our hope is that we are giving the learner control of their learning. But I doubt I am the only one who wonders about the level of engagement when their learners are looking at a computer screen. Even with the best intentions, simply dropping emergent technology into an existing system and expecting the same experience and outcomes is unrealistic. We must do our best to fully understand our culture and how a potential innovation will affect it. Our journey is rife with inevitable change, but laying out our map by planning for meaningful adoption can help us navigate that change more successfully and avoid major drawbacks.

To identify gaps and the potential need for change, we can use a simple needs assessment.

Needs Assessment

- What is our current situation? (What do we know?)
- Where do we want to be with potential changes? (What do we *want* to know?)
- What indicators will help us know if we are having success? (What are we trying to measure, determine, or define?)
- How can we keep track of these indicators? (How will we collect and record information?)
- How will we use indicators to identify success and failures in order to plan forward? (How will we report the information we record?)
- Have we heard from everyone who is impacted by the potential change? (Are all interested groups included in planning? Could we conduct a needs assessment in a group format?)

How Culture Is Developed

We can better plan where we want to go when we understand the culture. Culture is not innate. We are not born with it; we create it—together. According to researchers, culture has five basic characteristics: learned, shared, based on symbols, integrated, and dynamic.[48] All cultures share these basic characteristics.

- **Culture is learned**. It is not biological; we do not inherit it. Much of learning culture is unconscious. We learn culture from families, peers, institutions, and media. The process of learning culture is known as enculturation.
- **Culture is shared**. Despite the fact everyone is different—even within the same culture—culture is shared, and people share

enough to exist together. They can act in socially appropriate ways (according to their culture) as well as predict how others will act.

- **Culture is based on symbols.** A symbol is something that stands for something else. Symbols vary cross-culturally and are arbitrary. They only have meaning when people in a culture agree on their use. Language, money, and art are all symbols. Language is the most important symbolic component of culture.
- **Culture is integrated.** The various parts of a culture are interconnected. All aspects of a culture are related to one another, and to truly understand a culture, one must learn about all of its parts—not only a few.
- **Culture is dynamic.** Because most cultures are in contact with other cultures, they exchange ideas and symbols. These interactions cause cultures to change. All cultures change to be able to adapt to changing environments.

To promote a positive culture that is ready to change, we must work to create a *dynamic equilibrium* with dialogue and shared understanding driving our decision. Dynamic equilibrium is when a culture accepts change and is able to adapt. This occurs when the rate of change in culture is at a rate that is related to the culture's ability to cope with it.

The ability to cope with change is not fixed. We can change it for the positive or the negative. With purposeful intent and action, we can grow our togetherness, become more resilient to change, and be more capable of accepting change as a constant. In other words, we can promote a real culture of innovation and start a positive culture shift.

The N-S-E-W Positive Culture Shift

Sometimes, a positive culture shift is as simple as disrupting our status quo and trying something new. For example, invite students into your classroom for lunch and ask them to select the music, play a game, or just enjoy each other's company with no discussion about "school work." I have personally found this very rewarding. Appreciating each other's humanness is incredibly important.

The N-S-E-W Positive Culture Shift practices can further lead to an inclusive culture that values voice and choice and understands that change is inevitable. N-S-E-W will support our culture's ability to cope with change by balancing our dynamic equilibrium as we navigate the uncertain journey on which we embark. Culture can be and should be shaped through deliberate effort. To do so, we must be deliberate in our course for a positive culture shift and start to practice several simple things:

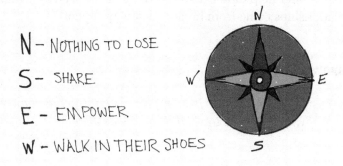

N - NOTHING TO LOSE

S - SHARE

E - EMPOWER

W - WALK IN THEIR SHOES

N - Nothing to Lose

The real voyage of discovery consists not in seeking new landscapes,
but in having new eyes.
—Marcel Proust[49]

Approach each lesson and each training with fresh eyes and the belief that you have nothing to lose and everything to gain by providing a new experience to others. Try new things, don't give up, and if you fail at first—employ a little "reckless abandon."

S - Share

Traveling—it leaves you speechless, then turns you into a storyteller.
—Ibn Battuta[50]

Sharing is one of the most valuable parts of the journey: sharing whom you met, what you saw, how you felt, what you learned. Sharing your successes and failures not only deepens your understanding of the experience but informs others and, perhaps, spawns new and better ideas. By sharing with our colleagues (our PLC, PLN, and our communities), we find support to continue and we encourage others to push themselves as well. The idea that we should only offer help rather than receive it can be seen as arrogant. Real relationships come from honest, two-way support.

E - Empower

The pleasure we derive from journeys is perhaps dependent more on the mindset with which we travel than on the destination we travel to.
—Alain de Botton[51]

Give voice to learners and colleagues alike. Participate in and support a culture of listening and of productive dialogue.

W - Walk in Their Shoes

The fundamental human experience is that of compassion.
—Joseph Campbell[52]

Real, true empathy means relating to lived experience. In our classrooms, we can recall the teacher that made a real difference in our own lives and translate that to how we interact with our learners. As learners, we know what kind of instruction we prefer. Perhaps our own learners feel the same way.

Waypoint #5

 Reflect on N-S-E-W. How can you practice these your next day of school? Take a few minutes to describe what you can do to leverage these practices immediately.

Nothing to Lose:

Share:

Empower:

Walk in Their Shoes:

Signpost #6: Community

Community is comprised of people, a culture, who share the same general mission and the same set of social meanings relevant to their context. Our mission must include the voice of learners, teachers, administration, and parents.

How are we giving voice to each? Where and how can each be heard as it pertains to decision-making in our schools?

Learners:

Teachers:

Administration:

Parents:

Further, our community includes future employers. How do we allow career readiness to be informed? In other words, do we have a place for future employers to voice concerns about career readiness gaps?

Signpost #7: Division of Labor

 Division of labor refers to the work requirements within our school culture. What types of jobs exist (faculty, staff, and so on)? What are the job titles used? Who makes decisions for curriculum, technology, staffing, and other areas?

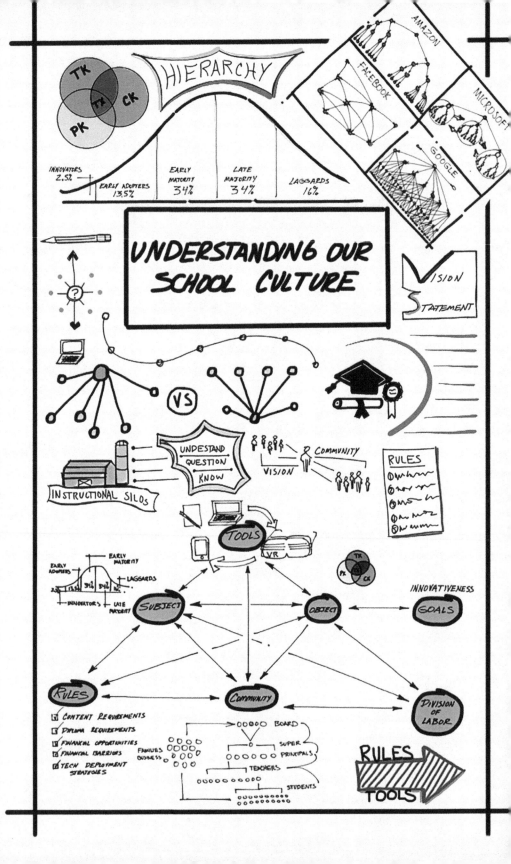

Understanding Our School Culture

The productivity of a work group seems to depend on how the group members see their own goals in relation to the goals of the organization.
—Paul Hersey and Kenneth H. Blanchard

Have you ever stood in front of a class of students and thought, *I'm so glad they don't realize there are way more of them than me?* Or even worse, *Oh no, I've lost control! What do I do now?* I have found it is best to keep these thoughts on the inside!

These thoughts show the reality that a small authoritarian rulership (administrators and teachers) oversees a body of free people (students) who have little to no voice in decisions. The common people vastly outnumber their "oppressive" rulers, yet we find relatively few uprisings. Sounds like the making of a dystopian young adult novel.

My point is that school culture and "status quo" guide and control us far more than we might realize. That's not a bad thing, any more than a small group of teachers and administrators running a large school is a bad thing. The way we think about schools in terms of a hierarchy can, of course, support certain levels of efficiency, but it is imperative that we do not allow this structure to define us and box us in. Just because "that's the way we've always done it" doesn't mean that's the way it *must* be done.

Our most basic school organizational structures have direct reporting lines that operate with certain levels of interaction between school administrators, teachers, students, parents, and our communities.[1] These

99

interactions, particularly the lateral ones, often do little to support or encourage interdisciplinary instruction. As a result, they can propagate one of the greatest detriments of modern education: silos.

Silos, or cross-content barriers, illustrate industrial revolution thinking, which focused on preparing an individual for a certain task in a certain place. Think of a traditional assembly line where a worker adds one single widget to one machine. They do this as they have been trained to do with no real comprehension of all of the moving parts. If we lack interdisciplinary instruction or vision, we can end up training our learners to do the same: to focus on their one widget and not worry about how the whole system works.

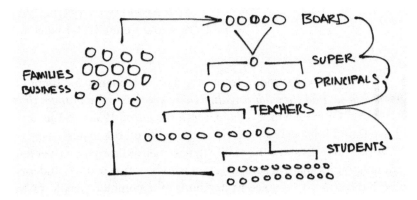

Conway's Law

According to Conway's Law, the lines by which we explain our interactions with each other can tell us about ourselves.[53] An organizational system built on sharing and collaboration will look very different than an organization system which fosters a competitive atmosphere. Take, for example, this unofficial look at Amazon, Microsoft, Facebook, and Google.[53b]

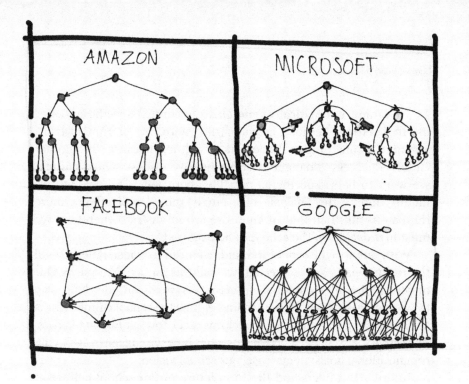

What would a review of our school hierarchical structures look like? Would we be Amazon, Microsoft, Facebook, or Google? Would we see instructional silos that limit our collaboration? Would an exploration of our school schedules reveal a case of pervasive isolation? If so, we have just identified a barrier in growing a culture of innovativeness. If this is the case, we have to spend time developing and establishing our shared cultural norms and our shared beliefs about school.

The Activity System

In education, we develop school-wide vision statements that explain our educational focus (our intended destination) and mission statements to explain how we're going to get there. The process of mapping out how we function should take into account all the activity that goes on in our school while accurately reflecting who we are.

The word "activity" can be used in a more technical sense to describe a cultural phenomenon which is unique to each school context. This is sometimes referred to as activity theory.[54]

We cannot automatically generalize our context-specific activities to other settings because, as we learned with the Yir Yamont tribe, assuming something will benefit a culture because of another culture's success is dangerous. So when we discuss school culture, we want to be as specific as possible about what "school" we are talking about. The analysis of a single school will offer a more intimate result than that of an entire school district. Therefore, we must first decide on the school to be explored.

With our specific school in mind, we need to understand how all the moving parts are connected; we call this an *activity system*. Our understanding of a school as an activity system can go a long way toward increasing our understanding of how the school culture works and, more importantly, how to help us steer toward innovativeness. The activity system perspective illustrates how we engage in achieving organizational goals: in our case, our school vision.

In order to understand the full picture of our school culture at work, the activity system, we must understand that it includes the subject(s), object, outcome, tools, community, rules, and division of labor, as well as how they are interconnected. This provides us with a critical lens, a context-analysis template, to investigate the unique activity of innovation adoption within our school culture. In short, we can better understand our rich journey by exploring it with this magnifying glass called the activity system.[55]

The many moving parts each dynamically contribute to the school vision we hope to achieve. This can be applied to any school vision, but the vision we've been addressing in this book is a school culture that embraces innovativeness. To make full sense and use of the activity system concept, we must describe the various components involved (see the School Culture Analysis Chart later on).

 Here is where our chapter signposts come into play. Each one has been guiding us to this point, to our goal, our *vision statement* which explains our school's focus to embrace innovativeness. Let's review what each signpost told us.

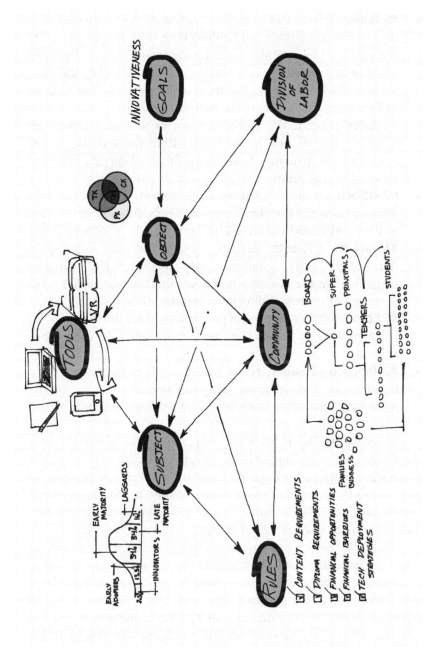

- **#1 Tools:** can be methods employed and/or the devices (technology) used by the subjects toward fulfilling their work requirements. We not only use tools, we also continuously renew and develop them, whether consciously or not. Further, we not only obey the rules, we also mold and reformulate them while we work. The tools are as dynamic a part as any to the Activity System.
- **#2 Rules:** refers to the regulations, norms, and conventions that constrain actions and interactions within the activity system. Economically speaking, these are the financial opportunities and limitations that inform a school's activity process.
- **#3 Object:** for our innovativeness discussion, the object is for a school community to embrace innovativeness. This can relate to how well we understand and are able to work with the TPACK model.
- **#4 and #5 Subjects:** describe faculty and staff as adopters (innovators, early adopters, early majority, late majority, laggards). We need to list who fits within these categories when framing our understanding around innovation.
- **#6 Community:** comprised of people who share the same general mission, who share a set of social meanings relevant to their context.
- **#7 Division of Labor:** refers to the work requirements to be fulfilled by the subjects. The functionality of a school's hierarchical structure is a school's own cultural phenomenon.

Our signposts have been our stopping points along the way, directing us and contributing to our effectiveness. The activity system approach illustrates how the multiple variables in our schools are involved in the success or failure of our vision. It provides a map to investigate the activity of innovation adoption within an organization and gives us an overview of our living, breathing school culture.

Schools are not stagnant or totally predictable. Like any evolving thing, we make constant adjustments to make sure they are accurately reflecting our context. Imagine looking up a place on Google Earth and finding there was an error. You would fix it, replace it, and/or report the error. So it is with our activity system, and so it is with our schools. *Reiteration*, *reformation*, and *redefining* are crucial to the design and development of school cultures embracing innovativeness.[56]

And if, or dare I say *when,* we get lost on our journey, and panic sets in, and unsettling questions riddle our minds, we should be prepared. Anyone who has been lost, whether in the forest or the mall, can relate. Actually, the U.S. Forest Service has some fitting advice using their STOP acronym, which I've summarized here.[57]

S - STOP: as soon as you realize you may be lost, just *stop.* Stay calm. Panic is your greatest enemy.

T - THINK: go over in your mind how you got to where you are. What landmarks should you be able to see?

O - OBSERVE: get your compass and determine the direction to take. Do not walk aimlessly. If you are on a trail, stay on it. If you must, follow a stream downhill; it can be difficult but often leads to a trail or road.

P - PLAN: based on your thinking and observations, come up with some possible plans. It is best not to take action until you have an informed plan.

Hopefully, you are no longer a solo traveler and you have your PLC and PLN in place. Reach out to them. They are out there, and they are a powerful tool! You are not alone, nor are you the first person to take this journey. Get help! Maybe you are used to being a doer, helper, and fixer, but you also need to be willing to receive help when you need it. Showing that you need help will only strengthen your relationships.

Waypoint #6

Think through the components of the activity system concept[58,59] to frame powerful insights into your school culture. Complete the School Culture Analysis Chart, putting together your signposts with a new understanding of an activity system's components.

School Culture Analysis Chart

Goal	Vision: what will be produced?	Innovativeness
Community	How would you describe your school community? Locally? Regionally? How are they connected?	Building(s): District: Region: Organizational hierarchy:
Object	What types of interventions might work to help create a culture of innovation?	
Rules	Content area requirements? Diploma fulfillment requirements? Financial opportunities and barriers to adopting emerging technology? Technology deployment strategy?	
Division of Labor	What does your school's organizational hierarchy look like? (Who are people accountable to?)	
Tools	What technology-based solutions are available? (hardware and software) What learning environments are available?	Devices (hardware) Apps/extensions (software) Open rooms/flexible spaces
Subjects	Who are the people in your school?	Innovators: Early adopters: Early majority: Late majority: Laggards:

School Culture Analysis Chart

Once you identify the different components of your school culture, it is time to dive in. Perhaps the most important piece to this cultural analysis puzzle is how each part interacts. Look back at the Activity System chart. The arrowed lines that connect each of the components are meant to push us to investigate more than just who or what is in place. Look at the lines and ask yourself the following:[60,61]

- Does the *community* actually inform *tool* adoption and expectations?
- Do *subjects* have the ability to take risks and try new things, or are they confined to their jobs as described in the *division of labor*? What are the approval channels for faculty and staff to innovate?
- Can *subjects* inform the adoption of specific *tools*? How?
- Do the *rules* and *community* allow/want *subjects* to adopt emergent technology?
- Do the actual activities of adopters match up with the *division of labor*? Are there reporting gaps?
- *Tools* change over time. What funding is in place to support this? What funding can be pursued?
- Who has a voice in the decision-making process?
  - Parents?
  - Teachers?
  - Students?
  - Administrators?
  - School board?
  - The workforce?
- Whose voice is not heard?

We can now use the activity system model to summarize our school culture in terms of how we are achieving our goal(s). We can also use the activity system model to see where our gaps or contradictions, are—that is, the way things look versus how they actually function. Don't be frustrated if you find contradictions, because they are critical to the innovation adoption process. Contradictions are the moving force, the disruption necessary, for the change and development of the system.[62] When contradictions come to the surface, we can expect some of our adopters to begin to question and deviate from our established norms, which is just the change we often need. Contradictions can grow into collaboration and a deliberate collective change effort.[63]

Signpost #8: Contradictions and School Culture Analysis

Contradictions: After you have completed the School Culture Analysis Chart, reflect on the weaknesses in the chart. Where are the connecting arrows not actually functioning as they should? What can you learn?

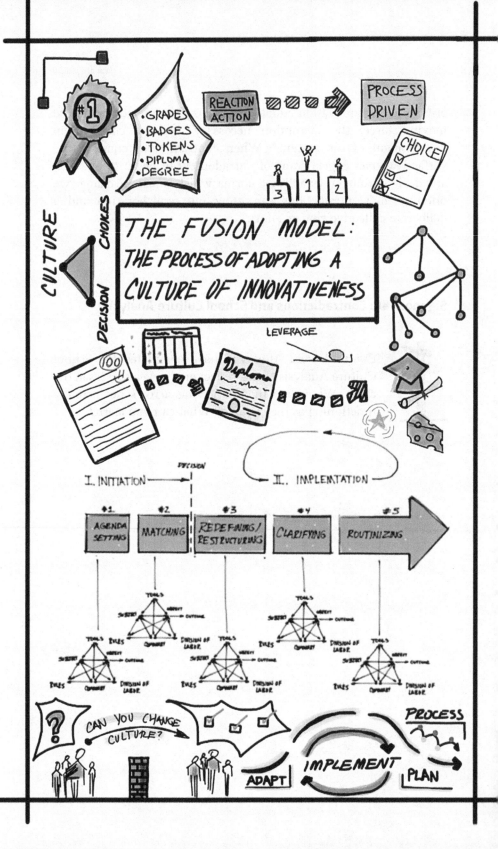

The Fusion Model: The Process of Adopting a Culture of Innovativeness

Let's do this!
—Leeroy Jenkins

uman nature drives us to identify when we have *arrived.* Grades, badges, certifications, and degrees are all an attempt to illustrate accomplishment. We want validation that we have made it. I have collaborated with schools and colleagues who seek to know, assess, and measure achievement. They want to know, *Are we doing it right?* They want checklists, rubrics, and other measurements for administrators to assess whether or not their school has fully adopted emergent technology in one way or another.

Such measurements exist, but I propose that perhaps we should adjust how we think about them. Remember the peak baggers! Are you focused on the checklist, on completing a singular task, or are you focused on the whole, beautiful journey? A culture of innovativeness is a culture that accepts change as its only constant. Innovativeness is about the process and the journey—not the finish line.

In our journey to innovate, our efforts to establish a new cultural norm that embraces innovation start with individuals. To move from an individual, SAMR-type implementation to an innovative school culture is a broader-picture process. If we have mapped out the lay of the land earlier—via our activity system analysis—we are better prepared for success. Our last waypoint, the School Culture Analysis

Chart, provided us with a critical lens, a snapshot of what exists in our school. Our last signpost, Contradictions, had us examine how each of the activity system components (the previous signposts) interacted with each other.

Next, we will put it all together and explore our journey as a continuing story, a chronology that longitudinally unfolds. Our tool for this next step is the Fusion Model. The Fusion Model is an innovation technique I have developed over the years that allows us to better explain, predict, and account for the organizational factors that impede or facilitate the spreading, or diffusion, of innovativeness. The Fusion Model fuses the waypoints and signposts we have created with an understanding of the stages of the innovation process in an organization. These stages will help us describe what is happening in our schools as we build a culture of innovativeness, a culture that embraces change and understands the repetitive nature of the process.

The Innovation Process

The Fusion Model is a continuation of the mapping efforts on our journey. Before we launch into that step, however, we need to discover the process organizations go through when adopting an innovation. These can be divided into two main phases: the initiation phase and the implementation phase.

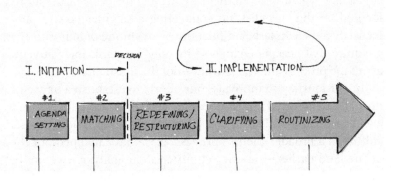

Initiation Phase

When we choose to begin our journey, we are in an initiation phase. Here we set our *agenda* and begin to *match* our findings with our purpose (see chart above). Because most innovations derive from an attempt to solve a problem, the *agenda* is our way of describing that there is a need for change. During this period, it can be meaningful to reflect on how we get to each step. Time allows the most insightful perspectives which can wisely inform next steps. Remember it is crucial to update our activity system evaluation regularly to reflect the impact an innovation is having. This will help us pinpoint what is working and what isn't. Do not assume other people on your journey are taking care of these updates. "I thought you were navigating" is a sure way to get lost.

Next, we explore innovations that we believe *match* our need. Remember, an innovation can include a tool or strategy. Once we decide what innovation we think is best to proceed, we move to the implementation phase.[66]

Implementation Phase

Implementing an innovation begins with *redefining/restructuring* the innovation to fit our structure. Because innovation is a disruptor that can lead to change at many levels, including our routines, processes, and practices, we must prepare for the fact that our school hierarchy might change as well.

As we progress through the implementation phase of an innovation, we next *clarify*. What will implementing look like? What will change? How will it be implemented? This also includes how the innovation is perceived, or defined, by our school culture.

Finally, when we no longer think of an innovation as independent of our school identity, we have *routinized* the innovation, and it is simply part of what we do.[67] That is to say, the innovation we have implemented no longer feels foreign, but it is now the norm of how our community operates.

Perhaps the easiest way to understand the innovation process in action is through an example or case study.

School 1234: A Case Study

Imagine a school anywhere in the world. We'll call it School 1234. The administration believes the school needs to demonstrate more eco-friendly practices as an example to its students and community. The school, of course, wants this to be in alignment with their already established future-ready goals. Here is how School 1234 would progress through the innovation process stages:

Agenda-Setting
To achieve this, the administration begins to pursue a goal of going paperless. The administration wants the changes they pursue to match their existing desire to prepare students for their future.

Matching
After investigating best practices, the administration believes a 1:1 device program will be the direction to pursue. Teachers identified as innovators and early adopters are brought into the dialogue to flush out initial concerns. There is a need for professional development due to the impending disruption.

Redefining/Restructuring
The rollout of 1:1 devices occurs. Teachers and students are provided with devices and bandwidth to technically go paperless. Professional development opportunities are provided to help with a pedagogy shift. Innovators, early adopters, and early majority attend the training sessions.

Clarifying
The administration announces it will stop purchasing/supporting print media. No more photocopiers, no more ink, no more printers (ouch!). The administration has demonstrated they are "all in" on

their paperless agenda. Professional development is mandated to support late adopters and laggards with the tools necessary to shift pedagogy to match the instructional need.

Routinizing
As a result, being paperless and 1:1 become ongoing elements of School 1234. Both are viewed as just the way they do things: "business as usual." The norm for their school culture has shifted.

Further Exploration with the Activity System

You've set your *agenda* and *matched* it with a proper tool or strategy. You *redefined* and *restructured* how it will fit in your school and what changes to expect. The school understands what the rollout will look like and the administration has *clarified* that they are supporting this innovation. And finally, this innovation is *routine* and normal. School 1234 is done innovating, right?

No! To sustain a culture of innovativeness, a school must build a system that allows for a voice from all stakeholders: teachers, students, parents, and community. Voices must be heard as schools seek to serve and innovate. A sustainable level of innovativeness:

- understands that we will be constantly redefining and reinventing
- promotes access and employment of meaningful technology
- finds, embraces, and elevates their champions

Let's add the activity system model[68] to the equation to get a much richer explanation of what is going on and what shifts occur. The activity system concept combined with the innovation process gives us an excellent way to dissect the interactivity involved with all that is going on around our school's choice to innovate. This is what I call the Fusion Model.

The Fusion Model: School 1234 Going Paperless

Activity System	I. INITIATION ⟶		Decision - - - →	II. IMPLEMENTATION ⟶	
	#1 Agenda-Setting	**#2 Matching**	**#3 Redefining/ Restructuring**	**#4 Clarifying**	**#5 Routinizing**
Goal	• Eco-Friendly • Future Ready	• Eco-Friendly • Future Ready	• Eco-Friendly • Future Ready	• Eco-Friendly • Future Ready	• Eco-Friendly • Future Ready
Community	• K-12	• K-12	• K-12	• K-12	• K-12
Objects		• Teacher Advisory Team	• 1:1 Professional Development	• 1:1 Professional Development	• 1:1 Professional Development
Rules	• Report Cards printed every 5 weeks.	• Report Cards printed every 5 weeks.	• Report Cards printed every 5 weeks. • Online Grading every 5 weeks	• Online Grading updated every two weeks	• Online Grading updated regularly
Division of Labor	• Photocopy Repairman - Contracted • Contracted IT support	• Photocopy Repairman - Contracted • Contracted IT support	• Photocopy Repairman - Contracted • Full-Time IT support	• Full-Time IT support	• Full-Time IT support • Advisory (voice) team: Teachers, Students, Parents, Administrators
Tools	• Pencil • Paper	• *Pencil* • *Paper* • *1:1 Devices*	• Pencil • Paper • 1:1 Devices	• 1:1 Devices	• 1:1 Devices
Subjects	• Teachers • Students	• Teachers • Students	• Teachers • Students	• Teachers • Students	• Teachers • Students

From here, we explore the impact on our school activity. Evaluating the entire activity system allows us to discern each stage and describe the variables that will have an impact on achieving our objectives. Furthermore, when one adjustment to an activity system component (signpost) occurs, it affects the relationship each component has with the other.

For example, in the chart, when 1:1 devices (tools) are introduced, the school will require a more robust IT department but will also require less photocopy support. This is a shift in the division of labor, as illustrated in the shaded boxes in the School 1234 chart.

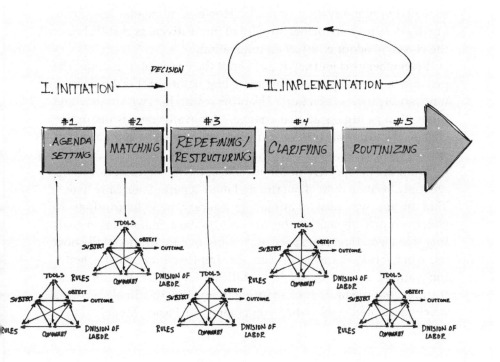

Employing the Fusion Model Is Iterative

Our schools are more dynamic than many of us are comfortable to admit. The world around us is rapidly changing, and it is directly impacting what our students experience outside of school and what is relevant to them. This dynamic condition means our school cultures are constantly changing, and we need to change with them (even if that makes us uncomfortable). "We have always done things this way" is not a reason to not innovate.

It is up to every single one of us to choose whether or not to meaningfully adopt emergent technology. We will sometimes find ourselves the recipients of what my colleagues and I jokingly call "shared-decision making": decisions are made and then shared with us. Not a very motivating situation! However, no matter how, who, or why decisions are made, the core of innovativeness is still choice: the choice to adopt or reject an innovation.

Remember, this journey is not about the endpoint, it is about the process—a true adventure. The unsettling nature of this diffusion of innovation process is supported by other researchers who understand innovation as organizational change.[69] Innovativeness is disruptive change, a journey of constant iteration, and it must be approached as such.

From the perspective of Moore's Law, technological innovations will only become more powerful and more a part of our daily lives.[70] That means we must continue to leverage new innovations to effectively and efficiently achieve instructional communication goals that transcend time and space. Revisiting one innovation will show us where that innovation can be improved or where better innovations can be made. It is difficult to predict the future of learning, but the process of adopting innovation in schools becomes much more predictable when you employ the Fusion Model.

Waypoint #7

Consider your own context. What initiatives are you involved in? What is coming? Complete the Fusion Model chart to support your understanding of where you have been and where you are going.

The Fusion Model

Activity System	#1 Agenda-Setting	#2 Matching	#3 Redefining/ Restructuring	#4 Clarifying	#5 Routinizing
Goal	•	•	•	•	•
Community	•	•	•	•	•
Objects	•	•	•	•	•
Rules	•	•	•	•	•
Division of Labor	•	•	•	•	•
Tools	•	•	•	•	•
Subjects	•	•	•	•	•

I. INITIATION — Decision — II. IMPLEMENTATION

Signpost #9: Get Involved

Get involved: If you are not involved in initiatives at your school, where can you have a voice to promote positive change? If you are involved, where can you extend your voice to promote positive change?

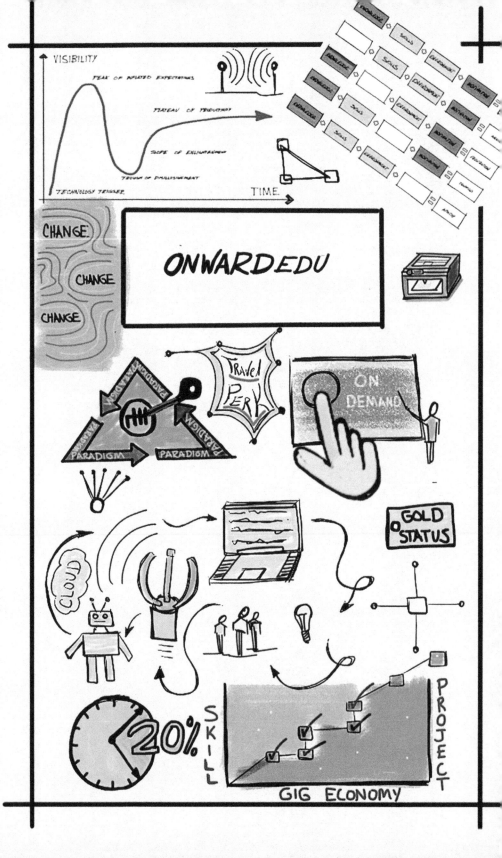

OnwardEDU

*Man cannot discover new oceans unlesshe has
the courage to lose sight of the shore.*
—Andre Gide

R emember your child-like wonder about the future? Anything
was possible. All the possibilities were exciting. The future
truly *can* be that way, though how we frame our thinking
toward the unknown affects the outcome. Personally, I am optimistic
about breakthroughs in emergent technology that will provide our
students with increased access to amazing learning opportunities,
like the virtual reality (VR) universe described by author Ernest
Cline in his book *Ready Player One*:

> During our World History lesson that morning, Mr.
> Avenovich loaded up a stand-alone simulation so that our
> class could witness the discovery of King Tut's tomb by
> archaeologists in Egypt in AD 1922. (The day before, we'd
> visited the same spot in 1334 BC and had seen
> Tutankhamen's empire in all its glory.)
>   In my next class, Biology, we traveled through a human
> heart and watched it pumping from the inside, just like in
> that old movie, *Fantastic Voyage.*
>   In Art class we toured the Louvre while all of our
> avatars wore silly berets.
>   In my Astronomy class we visited each of Jupiter's
> moons. We stood on the volcanic surface of Io while our

123

teacher explained how the moon had originally formed. As our teacher spoke to us, Jupiter loomed behind her, filling half the sky, its Great Red Spot churning slowly just over her left shoulder. Then she snapped her fingers and we were standing on Europa, discussing the possibility of extraterrestrial life beneath the moon's icy crust.[71]

Think about how awesome it *will* be to take students on journeys like this. And notice the *"we"*-ness of the account. While it is a fictional-futurist account, Cline references an important aspect of a successful, widespread, educational, *shared* experience. In each of the fictional high school courses found above, the main character attends virtual reality classes and goes on virtual experiences with his classmates. I see some very powerful educational applications for VR field trips where all students are immersed in the learning context together and a reflective review can occur to dissect both the content and the social interactions that occur in the learning. But we must understand that for these powerful, virtual opportunities to occur in a classroom, we must be prepared to shift our practice.

Further, augmented reality (AR) continues to become a powerful learning medium. AR differs from VR in that AR adds three-dimensional imagery directly into your real-world view (versus VR which transports you somewhere else virtually). In my social studies classes, I have leveraged AR in some interesting ways. Using Google Expeditions, and allowing students to bring their own devices to class, we examined the world of the Renaissance. I brought my students outside and connected all of our devices together through a wireless router, allowing us to share in one Google Expedition outside of our school building.

In this short-distance field trip, my students and I examined Leonardo da Vinci's machines in AR. The machines were added to our real-world view through our devices, allowing us to walk around them and step closer for better viewing. I was struck by how the context of our learning really contributed to what they were seeing. My students were able to see natural resources everywhere—trees, dirt, sand, and grass—and then look at three-dimensional computer-generated models of DaVinci's creations which used the same natural resources. What struck me is that students were given an in-the-moment experience that was related to their immediate surroundings. It allowed them to retain a sense of mindfulness and awareness of the environment in which the great Renaissance inventor was able to invent over five hundred years ago.[72]

VR and AR have come a long way over the past several years. In education, we now have applications which essentially bring paper to life and transport students to faraway places. Most of it is experienced individually; that is, individual users, on their own devices, have a unique experience. But imagine a future where VR and AR experiences are shared and social interaction is used in the meaning-making process. Exciting, right?

Considering Moore's Law again—that new technology is being produced at rapid speed and is becoming more available and accessible than ever before. The possibilities for helping students understand the power of technology and for preparing students for *their* future is endless. There is no reason we can't give our students everything they need (knowledge, skills, environment, and motivation) to be successful.

Performance Success Model

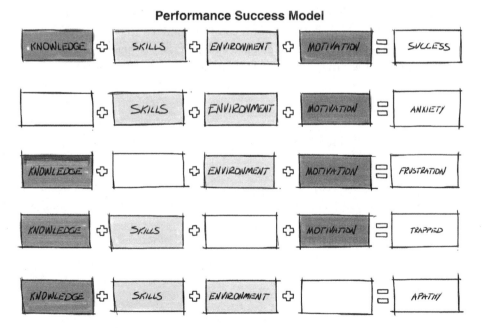

This adventure is cyclical. The realization that we embark on a constant state of change and a journey to innovate should be not just our mantra but our promise. We cannot grow while existing in silos of curriculum or with our classroom door closed to our community. We cannot build our schools on a foundation dependent on products or brands; technology is evolving too fast.

Open those doors. Strengthen your tribe. Accept the rapid change of technology. And get grounded in innovation.

Our objective as educators isn't just to engage our students by simply hooking them on entertaining or trending toys, but rather to immerse them in deep, meaningful insight. No matter how new and exciting emergent technology is, the true educational potential is only achieved through thoughtful experience design and purposeful conversation. So how can we make the most informed decisions about where to invest in the next steps?

Gartner Hype Cycle

There are resources available to us that identify rising patterns in emergent technology. One such resource is the Gartner Hype Cycle, an annual, graphical depiction of a common pattern that arises with tech-based innovation. It is often used by businesses to make decisions about technology investments.[73] So why not use it in education?

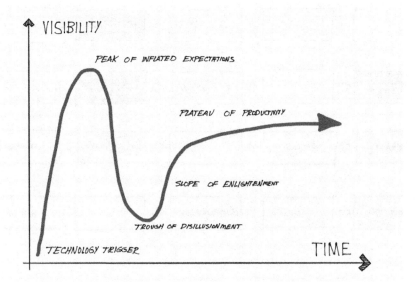

The Hype Cycle illustrates an innovation's growth and evolution in forward-moving time. There are identifiable phases which can help us understand when and if an innovation might be relevant to our context.

Technology trigger: A potential technology breakthrough launches. Early proof-of-concept stories and media interest trigger significant publicity (often no usable products exist yet).

Peak of inflated expectations: Early publicity produces a number of success stories, often accompanied by scores of failures. Expectations are at their highest.

Trough of disillusionment: Interest wanes as experiments and implementations fail to deliver. Producers of the technology demonstrate their ability to produce or they fail completely. Investment continues only if the surviving providers improve their products to the satisfaction of early adopters.

Slope of enlightenment: More instances of how the technology can fulfill a need appear (a perceived benefit), and the technology becomes more widely understood. Second-generation and third-generation products appear from technology providers.

Plateau of productivity: Mainstream adoption starts to take off. Innovators and early adopters are already expert users of the technology.

Exploring the Hype Cycle with an educational lens[74] provides many invaluable insights into the future of technology and how educational institutes can use it to their benefit. The Hype Cycle:
- monitors new and emerging technologies that we can use in cooperation with academics.
- helps find new ways to support teaching and learning through the use of technology.
- guides our conversations as we share teaching and learning experiences with the assistance of new technologies and resources.
- supports our innovation by using and adopting emerging technologies that will be meaningful to our context.

To take it one step further, beyond predictive tools like the Hype Cycle, we have to think back to the story about the steel ax and unintended consequences. No one would have suspected that introducing a more modern technology would have contributed to the breakdown of an entire society, but change is inevitable and perpetual. As the famous saying goes, "The only constant is change." Is it better to adapt once it arrives or prepare for it?

I think we would all agree—let's prepare. We need to recognize the decrease in demand for certain jobs as technology replaces automated tasks and equip ourselves. For example, what impact will emergent uses of 3D printed houses have on our society? Will we be able to provide much-needed shelter to more people? At the same time, will skilled craftsman become less in need? We must understand that emergent technology will have that effect on our standardized educational systems as well.

Schools as Access Points

For centuries, libraries and schools have provided access to knowledge in various ways. Has their job really shifted that much? Shouldn't we view providing access through libraries and schools to innovation in the form of new technology and new media?

Recently I took a virtual reality headset to my classroom to have my students try it out. There were lots of "oohs" and "aahs" and plenty of excitement about the experience. Inspired, I thought, *This is pretty neat.* So I took in some drones for my broadcast students, and I said "Hey, let's try this out and see what shooting video with drones looks like. Perhaps we can use it on our morning broadcast."

They were excited as well. They quickly learned how to fly them and then taught *me* about flying *my* drones. They showed me how drones can be efficient at capturing video.

In the case of both the virtual reality headset and the drones, I heard a reoccurring comment coming from my students: things like, "I need to go home and try to get one of these," or, "I need to tell my parents I want one of these for Christmas or for my birthday."

And honestly, that reaction bothered me. Isn't school the best place to bridge the digital access gap? Why should they go home to purchase these tools? That would just pass the financial burden on to parents. Schools and libraries should be places where access to knowledge is made possible, but today's access does not necessarily mean a book in print—it is also emergent technology. Shouldn't it be a priority to provide our students with access to innovation and to the tools that will be part of their future?

On-Demand Training: A Paradigm Shift

All the attributes that allow for a successful journey—motivation, environment, skills, and knowledge—if leveraged for our students' success, will result in students running to our class rather than running from our class each day. Relevance has a way of doing that (see the ARCS model).

We should aim for that. We should think about what exactly our students are producing and figure out how to be a part of that conversation. Are they using these increasingly powerful devices to promote social good (within and without the classroom walls)? Are our students using emergent technology to contribute to their communities?

We find ourselves in a direct position to responsibly guide students to consume and craft content that is meaningful and reliable. Author Daniel Boorstin (*The Discoverers*) wrote about the rise of "a mobile community of transient spectators" he called "tourists." As an educator, researcher, and learner, I cannot help but think of this through an educational lens. Our learners are the new "tourists" who can learn whenever they want and wherever they want without being in a traditional learning space. They use mobile technology in authentic contexts for real-world relevance and know how to use these services collaboratively and individually. They are becoming not just consumers of information but producers.

Think about the last home DIY project you did. If you used YouTube to help you, you saw this in action. Relevant, on-demand, in-the-moment training is available to us anywhere, anytime. Multiple media outlets, YouTubers, and DIYers are regularly adding how-to videos for very specific tasks and products.

So why is this a big deal? How does this impact our institutions of teaching and learning? More than a dozen companies, including Google, Apple, and IBM, are no longer requiring applicants to have college degrees.[75] When I heard that, it blew my mind. Talk about a disruption to our system. These companies have publicly recognized that their employees can get the exact training they need at any time, outside of our standardized educational system. Don't get me wrong. I'm not advocating that we completely dismantle our education system and watch YouTube all day. But why can't we take the best of in-the-moment, non-traditional training and find creative ways to integrate it within our current system of learning?

The Future of Work and the Gig-Based Economy

The forecast for our innovation journey is that over the next twenty years, we are likely to see one of the most significant disruptions to the workforce and work as we know it in recent memory[76]. In one revealing poll,[77] 54% of the US workforce said they are not confident their job will exist in twenty years[78]—a scary self-reflection that must inform our instructional practice.

Where is all of this change coming from? The demographic and socioeconomic trends of the past decade (such as rapid urbanization and globalization) coupled with even faster advances in technology (from mobile internet to increased automation) have caused a disruption like never before.[79] Are we preparing our students for this shift in the workplace?

Innovation goes beyond a simple new tool. Innovation infers application, capability, and methods of accomplishing a better workflow. The *future of work* (#FOW) will demand people are prepared to solve complex problems, interact with clients and colleagues, and adapt to new tools and workflows.

Further, the trend toward a "gig-based economy" has begun. A gig-based economy is defined as a way of working that is based on people having temporary jobs or doing separate pieces of work, each paid separately, rather than working for an employer.[80] A study by Intuit predicted that by 2020, 40% of American workers would be contributing to a gig economy as an independent contractor.[81] These contractors, developing their own brand in a feast-or-famine work atmosphere, must understand resilience, perseverance, and good old-fashioned stick-to-itiveness!

Clearly, a technology-driven shift in education is upon us. The future of work demands a different approach to the knowledge and skills we have relied on in the past. Our need to adopt emergent technology (and meaningful pedagogy to leverage it) has never been this high.

Pedagogical shifts must transcend simply integrating new technology in our instruction. We must adopt innovativeness in order to prepare our students for a gig-based economy where understanding and thriving in the constant state of change will help them ride out the dark valleys, knowing the mountaintops are coming.

The Ripple Effect of Change

If we try to innovate by ourselves, we are doomed. A team, a tribe, a cohort of adopters (at every stage) are all stakeholders in our school community. Each must be valued; each must be understood for who they are. Who knows exactly what skills will be required in the near future?

The changes we embark on should be driven by the needs our students will have to be successful for their future. We often think solely about emergent technology, but we must remember that innovation can come in multiple forms. Do we need to focus on keyboarding skills when voice typing is becoming so powerful? Do we need to focus on coding when AI is on the rise?

One thing will always remain, though: people, with their stories and their insights. No matter where technology goes, people will always be important—in the future more than ever. In 2018, Jeff

Weiner, the CEO of LinkedIn, stated that the number one most-lacking skill for Americans in the workplace was not coding: it was soft skills.[82]

Soft skills are the skills to collaborate and communicate. These skills allow a person to effectively interact with another or within a group. Jeff Weiner said, "Not surprisingly, there continues to be an imbalance with regards to software engineering. But somewhat surprisingly, the interpersonal skills area is where we're seeing the biggest imbalance. Communications is the number one skill gap."[83] One tool for soft skills development? Empathy, which we looked at earlier.

On our journey, we supply ourselves with new technology: instructional strategies, programs, and devices. But these are all just tools. Technology is not a silver bullet. In fact, technology is simply an amplifier—it will highlight both good and bad practice. Our shift must include a shift in pedagogy as part of the ripple effect of change.

Change is not easy. We must plan for it. We must communicate expectations and timelines in an effective manner. We have to leverage the insights, experience, and social power of our champions because even though change is necessary, not everyone is going to be as excited about it as you might be. Remember to have patience and be a communicator, a leader, and an empathizer.

And as we already saw, change is inevitable. The latest and greatest eventually gets old. (Remember fidget spinners?) Today's emergent technology will someday become obsolete or get recycled. Our pedagogy, our truest operating systems, must be updated to best meet the needs of our learners.

Wanderlusters with Travel Perks

Frequent travelers earn perks with airlines and other travel-related companies. But to get more perks, we have to invest more in travel. We have to do more. *Do more?* You might be asking yourself. *With what time?*

I have always been excited about the concept of "20% time" introduced in some corporate and educational institutions like

Google. It is "designed to give employees one full day per week (20 percent of their time) to work on a Google-related passion project of their own choosing or creation,"[84] and it might be the reason that Google is one of the most innovative companies in the world. But that's not often possible in the educational world, especially with the way our system is structured.

Most of us face the same limitations on our time, so we struggle with what to cut, where to cut it, and when to cut it in our quest to "do more." My solution to this conundrum is perhaps a bit unorthodox, but I assure you it has worked: I simply do more with what I have. I try to use my time as effectively and efficiently as I can. Pretty straightforward, right? Wherever and whenever I can, I find innovative ways to do more.

For example, I have decided to go paperless, cutting out forty-two hours a year standing at the photocopier. I have decided to eat my lunch with my students so we can talk about how our worlds are similar and different. I have decided to use my homeroom as a studio for doing a live morning broadcast.

Why have I made these decisions? Because the results of these and other incremental changes have inspired me and advanced my growth. Changes like these have helped me accrue more "mileage"—more time spent learning and growing with students and colleagues. It is an investment in people. Remember to travel with your head up and enjoy the view and the company.

And to provide you with some extrinsic motivation (because we know both intrinsic and extrinsic motivations are effective), there are also advantages to being innovative with our time—advantages like status. Airline travelers love status: the upgraded seat, the early boarding, the special treatment. All good stuff. In our journey as educators, we can identify with these perks when we reframe our thinking. Being innovative can offer:

- Upgraded seat: A desirable classroom in which we find students running *to* rather than running *from*. What is a desirable classroom? Well, that's up to you!
- Priority boarding: Gaining a reputation as a doer and a risk-taker will make you stand out and be recognized as valuable

to your colleagues—a sought-after asset. Be ready to help and be ready to be helped.

- Special treatment: The students will know you are interested in them, and they will take more interest in you! Relationships matter.

We aren't the first travelers to set off on a journey of adventure, innovation, and change. That is why, rather than just charting our own path and blazing uncharted trails, we have dug deep into practical research and models which allow us to better explain, predict, and adapt to the adoption of innovation.[85] It is my hope that you feel better equipped than ever for the journey ahead, full of meaningful skills, knowledge, and tools for the road.

Change is the one thing that never changes. Strategies and models will shift. Technology will evolve. So let innovativeness be your North Star, the constant that guides you.

About the Author

Micah Shippee, PhD, is a social studies teacher and educational technology trainer. He works to bridge the gap between research and practice in the educational sector. Micah explores ways to improve motivation in the classroom and seeks to leverage emergent technology to achieve educational goals. He is an innovative "ideas" person who likes to think and act outside the box. As an educational consultant and keynote speaker, he focuses on the adoption of emergent technology through the development of an innovative learning culture. Micah believes that innovativeness is the pedagogy of the future.

Chapter Source Notes

Introduction

Chapter quote: Anthony Bourdain. "No Reservations: Around the World on an Empty Stomach." BuzzFeed. "14 Times Anthony Bourdain Told Us Exactly What We Needed to Hear. BuzzFeed. n.d. Web. 26 Feb. 2019. www.buzzfeed.com/michelleno/anthony-bourdain-quotes-food-travel

[1] *Webster's New World College Dictionary, 4th Edition.* Copyright © 2010 by Houghton Mifflin Harcourt. All rights reserved.

[2] Shippee, Micah (2016) "mLearning in the Organizational Innovation Process." Dissertation. https://surface.syr.edu/etd/452. Note: In this original work, The Fusion Model is generically titled "Activity in the organizational innovation process."

Chapter 1

Chapter quote: J.R.R. Tolkien (2012). *The Lord of the Rings: One Volume,* p.169, Houghton Mifflin Harcourt

[3] https://www.merriam-webster.com/dictionary/technology. Accessed March 26, 2019.

[4] Britannica, The Editors of Encyclopaedia. Moore's Law. *Encyclopædia Britannica*, Encyclopædia Britannica, Inc., 29 Mar. 2019, www.britannica.com/technology/Moores-law.

[5] Meehan, K.C. and Salmun, H. "Integrating Technology In Today's Undergraduate Classrooms: A Look At Students' Perspectives." Digital. nsta.org. Journal of College Science Teaching, v46 n1 Sep 2016 Web. 15 Apr. 2019. http://digital.nsta.org/display_article.php?id=2558211&-view=329023

[6] Ganapati, P. WIRED. "June 4, 1977: VHS Comes to America." WIRED. 6 Jun. 2010. https://www.wired.com/2010/06/0604vhs-ces/. Accessed 8 Mar. 2018.

[7] "N.a. "Ohio School of the Air—Ohio History Central." Ohiohistorycentral. org. 16 Nov. 2017. http://www.ohiohistorycentral.org/w/Ohio_School_of_ the_Air. Accessed 28 Feb. 2018.

[8] Cuban, Larry. *Teachers and Machines: the Classroom Use of Technology since 1920.* Teachers College Press, 2004.

[9] Banks, Sarah, "A Historical Analysis of Attitudes toward the Use of Calculators in Junior High and High School Math Classrooms in the United States Since 1975" (2011). Master of Education Research Theses. 31. http://digitalcommons.cedarville.edu/education_theses/31

[10] Purdue University Online. "The Evolution of Technology in the Classroom." Purdue University Online. 8 Sept. 2014. https://online.purdue.edu/ ldt/learning-design-technology/resources/evolution-technology-classroom. Accessed 12 Apr. 2018.

[11] Shulman, L. (1987). "Knowledge and Teaching: Foundations of the New Reform." Harvard Educational Review, 57, 1–22.

[12] Frommer, Jake. "Common Traits of Gamers." Geeks.media. 14 Nov. 2016. https://geeks.media/common-traits-of-gamers Accessed 1 Jan. 2019.

[13] Ely, Donald P.. "ERIC—Conditions that Facilitate the Implementation of Educational Technology Innovations." Journal of Research on Computing in Education, 1990. Eric.ed.gov. n.d. Web. 28 Feb. 2019. https://eric.ed. gov/?id=EJ421756. Accessed 8 Mar. 2018.

Chapter 2

Chapter quote: William Arthur Ward. "A Quote by William Arthur Ward." Goodreads.com. https://www.goodreads.com/quotes/436006-if-you-can-imagine-it-you-can-achieve-it-if Accessed 26 Feb. 2019.

[14] John Masters, *Bugles and a Tiger: My Life in the Gurkhas;* Orion Pub Co (June 2002). Page 84.

[15] Harless, J.H. (1973). "An Analysis of Front-End Analysis. Improving Human Performance: A Research Quarterly," 4, 229-244. More about Dr. Joe Harless can be found in this short career biography http://exemplaryperformance.com/dr-joe-harless-honored-by-csg-board/ Accessed 2.20.2019

[16] "A Quote by Gaius Julius Caesar." Goodreads, 8 Mar. 2019, www.goodreads.com/quotes/308892-experience-is-the-teacher-of-all-things.

[17] "A Quote by Albert Einstein." Goodreads, www.goodreads.com/quotes/253933-i-never-teach-my-pupils-i-only-attempt-to-provide.

[18] Pereira CS, Teixeira J, Figueiredo P, Xavier J, Castro SL, Brattico E (2011) "Music and Emotions in the Brain: Familiarity Matters." PLoS ONE 6(11):

[19] Australian Council for Educational Research - ACER. "Classroom Layout—What Does the Research Say?" Australian Council for Educational Research - ACER. 16 Mar. 2017. <https://www.teachermagazine.com.au/articles/classroom-layout-what-does-the-research-say>. Accessed 7 Jun. 2018.

[20] "What Does Your Classroom Layout Say... - TES Teach with ... - Facebook." 15 Aug. 2016, https://www.facebook.com/TESTeachBlendspace/videos/857262131070472/. Accessed 7 Jun. 2018.

Chapter 3

Chapter quote: Billy Graham "A Time for Moral Courage," Reader's Digest (July 1964). "A quote by Billy Graham." Goodreads.com. https://www.goodreads.com/quotes/717403-courage-is-contagious-when-a-brave-man-takes-a-stand. Accessed 26 Feb. 2019.

[21] Darley, J. M. & Latané, B. (1968). "Bystander Intervention in Emergencies: Diffusion of Responsibility". Journal of Personality and Social Psychology. 8: 377–383. doi:10.1037/h0025589. https://pdfs.semanticscholar.org/9c2f/63826605843d83fd08f56fbf75790cf74614.pdf. Accessed 17 Apr. 2018.

[22] Howell, J., Shea, C., & Higgins, C. (2005). "Champions of Product Innovations: Defining, Developing, and Validating a Measure of Champion Behavior." Journal of Business Venturing, 20(5), 641-661.

[23] Greenhalgh, T., Robert, G., Macfarlane, F., Bate, P., & Kyriakidou, O. (2004). "Diffusion of Innovations in Service Organizations: Systematic Review and Recommendations." The Milbank Quarterly, 82(4), 581-629.

[24] Chart, titles, and statistics adapted from Rogers, E.M. (2003). *Diffusion of Innovations (5th ed.)*. New York: Free Press.

[25] Sivers, D. "Leadership Lessons from Dancing Guy | Derek Sivers." https://sivers.org/dancingguy. Accessed 17 Apr. 2018.

[26] Based on Rogers, E.M. (2003). *Diffusion of Innovations (5th ed.)*. New York: Free Press.

[27] Rogers, E.M. (2003). *Diffusion of Innovations (5th ed.)*. New York: Free Press.

Chapter 4

Chapter quote: Elbert Hubbard. "A Quote by Elbert Hubbard." Goodreads.com https://www.goodreads.com/quotes/319254-we-awaken-in-others-the-same-attitude-of-mind-we Accessed 26 Feb. 2019.

[28] Keller, J. (1987) Attention, Relevance, Confidence, and Satisfaction are developed in John Keller's ARCS model of motivational design.

[29] Kenton, W.. "Moore's Law." Investopedia. 11 Feb. 2019. <https://www.investopedia.com/terms/m/mooreslaw.asp>. Accessed 18 Apr. 2018.

[30] Buonarroti, Michelangelo. "A Quote by Michelangelo Buonarroti." Goodreads.com. N.d. Web 4 Apr. 2019. www.goodreads.com/quotes/557979-the-greatest-danger-for-most-of-us-is-not-that.

[31] Imber, Amantha. *Harvard Business Review.* "Help Employees Innovate by Giving Them the Right Challenge." 17 Oct. 2016. https://hbr.org/2016/10/help-employees-innovate-by-giving-them-the-right-challenge. Accessed 3 Jan. 2019.

[32] Tschannen-Moran, M. & Hoy, A.W. (2001) "Teacher Efficacy: Capturing an Elusive Construct, Teaching and Teacher Education." 17 (2001), pp. 783–805.

[33] Bandura, A. (1977). "Self-Efficacy: Toward a Unifying Theory of Behavioral Change." Psychological Review 84 (2), 191-215.

[34] Rogers, Everett M. *Diffusion of Innovations. 5th ed.* New York: Free, 2003. Print.

[35] Puentedura, R. "The SAMR Model." Hippasus.com. 8 Dec. 2010. http://hippasus.com/resources/sweden2010/SAMR_TPCK_IntroToAdvancedPractice.pdf. Accessed 28 Feb. 2019. See also https://en.wikiversity.org/wiki/Instructional_design/SAMR_Model/What_is_the_SAMR_Model%3F

[36] Based on: Schrock, K (2013) "SAMR - Kathy Schrock's Guide to Everything." 9 Nov. 2013, http://www.schrockguide.net/samr.html. Accessed 20 Apr. 2018.

[37] Based on Hord, S. M. (1997) "Professional Learning Communities: What Are They and Why Are They Important. Issues... about Change." 6 (1). Southwest Educational Development Laboratory (SEDL) Austin, Texas. http://www.sedl.org/pubs/change34/plc-cha34.pdf. Accessed April 17, 2019.

[38] Bandura, A. (1977). "Self-Efficacy: Toward a Unifying Theory of Behavioral Change." Psychological Review 84 (2), 191-215.

[39] Further explanation and details available at https://micahshippee.com/2011/09/28/pd-the-need-for-sharing/. Accessed April 17, 2019.

[40] DuFour, R. (2004) "What Is a 'Professional Learning Community'? Schools as Learning Communities." Educational Leadership 61(8)

[41] Shippee, M. & Dotger, B. (2010) "Perceptions of Success for Teachers: The Role of Mentor Programs." (unpublished).

[42] Ingersoll, R.M. (2003) "The Teacher Shortage: Myth or Reality?" Educational Horizons, 81 (3) (2003), 146–152.

[43] Smith, T.M. & Ingersoll, R.M. (2004). "What Are the Effects of Induction and Mentoring on Beginning Teacher Turnover?" American Education Research Journal 41 (3) (2004), pp. 681–714.

[44] Johnson, S.M. & Birkeland, S.E. (2003). "Pursuing a 'Sense of Success': New Teachers Explain Their Career Decisions." American Educational Research Journal 40 (3) (2003), pp. 581–617.

[45] Hanson, S (2010). "What Mentors Learn about Teaching." Educational Leadership, 67 (8) 2010, 76-80

[46] Reiman, A.J. & DeAngelis Peace, S. (2002) "Promoting Teachers' Moral Reasoning and Collaborative Inquiry Performance: a Developmental Role-Taking and Guided Inquiry Study." Journal of Moral Education, 31(1), 51-66.

Chapter 5

Chapter quote: Pico Iyer. "A Quote by Pico Iyer." Goodreads.com. https://www.goodreads.com/quotes/514173-a-person-susceptible-to-wanderlust-is-not-so-much-addicted. Accessed Web. 26 Feb. 2019

[47] Sharp, Lauriston (1952), "Steel Axes for Stone Age Australians," in Edward H. Spicer(ed.), Human Problems in Technological Change, New York, Russell Sage Foundation, pp. 69-72.

[48] Haviland, William A, Harald E. L. Prins, Bunny McBride, Dana Walrath, and William A. Haviland. "Cultural Anthropology: The Human Challenge." 2011. Print.

[49]"A Quote by Marcel Proust." Goodreads.com. www.goodreads.com/quotes/33702-the-real-voyage-of-discovery-consists-not-in-seeking-new. Accessed Web 26 Feb. 2019.

[50] Battuta, Ibn. "A Quote from The Travels of Ibn Battutah." Goodreads.com. www.goodreads.com/quotes/508820. Accessed Web. 26 Feb. 2019.

[51] de Botton, Alain. "A Quote from The Art of Travel." *Goodreads.com.* Accessed Web. 11 Apr. 2019, www.goodreads.com/quotes/622773.

[52] Campbell, Joseph. "A Quote from The Hero's Journey." *Goodreads.com.* Accessed Web 11 Apr. 2019. www.goodreads.com/quotes/7314898.

[53] Amrit, Chintan, Jos Hillegersberg, and Kuldeep Kumar. "A Social Network Perspective of Conway's Law." Proceedings of the CSCW Workshop on Social Networks, Chicago, IL, USA. 2004. https://www.utwente.nl/en/bms/iebis/staff/amrit/SocialNetworks-ConwaysLaw_latest.pdf

[53b] Cornet, M. "A Reimagined Illustration Based on the Work of Manu Cornet." Featured in the New York Times, Business Day section July 12, 2013. http://ma.nu/publications/images/2013.07.12_new_york_times_org_charts_small.png

Chapter 6

Chapter quote: Paul Hersey and Kenneth H Blanchard. Management of Organizational Behavior. "Full Text of 'Organizational Behavior—Second Edition.'" Archive.org. https://archive.org/stream/in.ernet.dli.2015.132797/2015.132797. Organizational-Behavior--second-Edition_djvu.txt. Accessed 26 Feb. 2019.

[54] Jonassen, D. H., & Rohrer-Murphy, L. (1999). "Activity Theory as a Framework for Designing Constructivist Learning Environments." Education Technology Research and Development, 47(I), 61–79.

[55] Engeström, Y. (2001). "Expansive Learning at Work: Toward an Activity Theoretical Reconceptualization." Journal of Education and Work, 14(1), 133–156. doi:10.1080/13639080020028747.

[56] Jonassen, D. H., & Rohrer-Murphy, L. (1999). "Activity Theory as a Framework for Designing Constructivist Learning Environments." Education Technology Research and Development, 47(I), 61–79.

[57] "If You Get Lost | US Forest Service." Fs.fed.us. https://www.fs.fed.us/visit/know-before-you-go/if-you-get-lost. Accessed 7 Jan. 2019.

[58] 1. Engeström, Y. (1996). "Developmental Studies of Work As a Testbench of Activity Theory: The Case of Primary Care Medical Practice." In S. Chaiklin & S. Lave (Eds.), "Understanding Practice: Perspectives on Activity and Context" (First., pp. 64–103). New York, NY: Cambridge University Press.

[59] Engeström, Y. (1987). "Learning by Expanding: An Activity-Theoretical Approach to Developmental Research." Helsinki: Orienta-Konsultit. Lchc. ucsd.edu. 27 Sept. 2011 Retrieved from http://lchc.ucsd.edu/mca/Paper/Engestrom/Learning-by-Expanding.pdf. Accessed 28 Feb. 2019.

[60] 4. Jonassen, D. H., & Rohrer-Murphy, L. (1999). "Activity Theory as a Framework for Designing Constructivist Learning Environments." Education Technology Research and Development, 47(I), 61–79.

[61] Engeström, Y. (1987). "Learning by Expanding: An Activity-Theoretical Approach to Developmental Research." Helsinki: Orienta-Konsultit. Lchc. ucsd.edu. 27 Sept. 2011 Retrieved from http://lchc.ucsd.edu/mca/Paper/Engestrom/Learning-by-Expanding.pdf. Accessed 28 Feb. 2019.

[62] Engeström, Y. (1996). "Developmental Studies of Work as a Testbench of Activity Theory: The Case of Primary Care Medical Practice." In S. Chaiklin & S. Lave (Eds.), "Understanding Practice: Perspectives on Activity and Context" (First., pp. 64–103). New York, NY: Cambridge University Press.

[63] Engeström, Y. (2001). "Expansive Learning at Work: Toward an Activity Theoretical Reconceptualization." Journal of Education and Work, 14(1), 133–156. doi:10.1080/13639080020028747.

Chapter 7

Chapter quote: Leeroy Jenkins (Aka Ben Schultz), World of Warcraft Wowpedia. "Leeroy Jenkins (video)." Wowpedia. https://wow.gamepedia. com/Leeroy_Jenkins_(video). Accessed 26 Feb. 2019.

[64] Shippee, Micah (2016) "mLearning in the Organizational Innovation Process." Dissertation. https://surface.syr.edu/etd/452 Note: In this original work, The Fusion Model is generically titled "Activity in the organizational innovation process."

[65] Rogers, E.M. (2003). *Diffusion of Innovations (5th ed.)*. New York: Free Press.

[66] Shippee, Micah (2016) "mLearning in the Organizational Innovation Process." Dissertation. https://surface.syr.edu/etd/452 Note: In this original work, The Fusion Model is generically titled "Activity in the organizational innovation process."

[67] Rogers, E.M. (2003). *Diffusion of Innovations (5th ed.)*. New York: Free Press.

[68] Rogers, E.M. (2003). *Diffusion of Innovations (5th ed.)*. New York: Free Press.

[69] Ally, M. (2009). "Mobile learning, Transforming the Delivery of Education and Training." Edmonton, AB, Canada: Au Pr.
—Cross, J. and Dublin, L. (2002). "Implementing eLearning." Alexandria, VA: ASTD
—Quinn, C. (2011). "Mobile learning: Landscape and Trends." The eLearning Guild. Santa Rosa, CA.

[70] Yoo, Y., Boland, R. J., Lyytinen, K., & Majchrzak, A. (2012). "Organizing for Innovation in the Digitized World." Organization Science, 23(5), 1398-1408. doi: 10.1287/orsc.1120.0771.

Chapter 8

Chapter quote: Andre Gide. Les faux-monnayeurs (The Counterfeiters). "A Quote by André Gide." Goodreads.com. https://www.goodreads.com/quotes/4661-man-cannot-discover-new-oceans-unless-he-has-the-courage. Accessed 26 Feb. 2019.

[71] Cline, Ernest. *Ready Player One*. Broadway Books, 2011.

[72] Micah Shippee. "Augmented Reality – The Art of BYOD in the Classroom." 16 Feb. 2019. https://micahshippee.com/2019/02/16/augmented-reality-the-art-of-byod-in-the-classroom/. Accessed 1 Mar. 2019

[73] Cleverism. "Everything You Need to Know about Gartner's Hype Cycle." Cleverism. 8 Jun. 2015. https://www.cleverism.com/everything-need-know-gartner-hype-cycle/. Accessed 10 Jan. 2019.

[74] Williams, K.C. "Hype Cycle for Education, 2017." Gartner.com. 24 Jul. 2017. https://www.gartner.com/doc/3769145/hype-cycle-education-. Accessed 10 Jan. 2019.

[75] Connley, Courtney. "Google, Apple and 12 Other Companies That No Longer Require Employees to Have a College Degree." CNBC. 16 Aug. 2018. https://www.cnbc.com/2018/08/16/15-companies-that-no-longer-require-employees-to-have-a-college-degree.html. Accessed 10 Jan. 2019.

[76] Tunkel, A. "Three Trends on the Future of Work." Forbes. 13 Aug. 2018. https://www.forbes.com/sites/forbesbusinessdevelopmentcouncil/2018/08/13/three-trends-on-the-future-of-work/. Accessed 8 Dec. 2018.

[77] Frey. C.B. and Osborne, M.A. "The Future of Employment: How Susceptible Are Jobs to Computerisation?" Sciencedirect.com. 29 Sept. 2016. Web. 22 Apr. 2019. <https://www.sciencedirect.com/science/article/pii/S0040162516302244?via%3Dihub>

[78] Inc., Wonolo. "Data on the Gig Economy and How It Is Transforming the Workforce." Wonolo. 15 Feb. 2018. https://www.wonolo.com/blog/data-gig-economy-transforming-workforce/. Accessed 8 Dec. 2018.

[79] Tunkel, A. "Three Trends on the Future of Work." Forbes. 13 Aug. 2018. https://www.forbes.com/sites/forbesbusinessdevelopmentcouncil/2018/08/13/three-trends-on-the-future-of-work/. Accessed 8 Dec. 2018.

[80] "GIG ECONOMY | definition in the Cambridge English Dictionary." Dictionary.cambridge.org. https://dictionary.cambridge.org/us/dictionary/english/gig-economy. Accessed 10 Jan. 2019.

[81] Rouse, M. "What Es Gig Economy? - Definition from WhatIs.com." WhatIs.com. https://whatis.techtarget.com/definition/gig-economy. Accessed 8 Dec. 2018.

[82] Umoh, Ruth. "The CEO of LinkedIn Shares the No. 1 Job Skill American Employees Are Lacking." CNBC. 26 Apr. 2018. https://www.cnbc.com/2018/04/26/linkedin-ceo-the-no-1-job-skill-american-employees-lack.html. Accessed 10 Jan. 2019.

[83] Laughter, C.G. "What Job Skill Is Most Lacking in the U.S.? LinkedIn CEO Jeff Weiner Has a Surprising Answer." American Employees are Lacking (sort of) 1 Surprising... | LinkedIn." Linkedin.com. 23 Aug. 2018. https://www.linkedin.com/pulse/what-job-skill-most-lacking-us-linkedin-ceo-jeff-weiner-c-g-laughter/. Accessed 1 Mar. 2019.

[84] Adams, Bryan. How Google's 20 Percent Rule Can Make You More Productive and Energetic." *Inc.com*, Inc., 28 Dec. 2016, www.inc.com/bryan-adams/12-ways-to-encourage-more-free-thinking-and-innovation-into-any-business.html.

[85] Cleverism. Everything You Need to Know about Gartner's Hype Cycle. Cleverism. 8 Jun. 2015. https://www.cleverism.com/everything-need-know-gartner-hype-cycle/. Accessed 10 Jan. 2019.

57502270R00086

Made in the USA
Middletown, DE
31 July 2019